REGIONAL WELL-BEING ACROSS KAZAKHSTAN

HARNESSING SURVEY DATA
FOR INCLUSIVE DEVELOPMENT

JUNE 2023

ADB

ASIAN DEVELOPMENT BANK

CONTENTS

TABLES, FIGURES, AND MAPS

Tables

Figures

Maps

ACKNOWLEDGMENTS

The *Regional Well-Being across Kazakhstan: Harnessing Survey Data for Inclusive Development* publication was prepared under the auspices of the Joint Government of Kazakhstan and the Asian Development Bank (ADB) Knowledge and Experience Exchange Program, Phase 4 (TA 6623-KAZ).

Andrés Rodríguez-Pose, Princesa de Asturias chair and professor of economic geography at the London School of Economics and Political Science, led the study with the support and co-authorship of Federico Bartalucci, economic development consultant. Genadiy Rau, senior economics officer, ADB Kazakhstan Resident Mission; and Kaisar Nigmetov, director of the Center for Regional Studies of Economic Research Institute under the Ministry of National Economy of the Republic of Kazakhstan, participated in the design of the research and provided oversight and support, both during the collection of data and drafting process.

We express gratitude to the staff of the Economic Research Institute who collected data and conducted the survey across Kazakhstan. April-Marie Gallega coordinated the editorial and publication process with the following ADB consultants: Layla Amar (copyediting), Lawrence Casiraya (proofreading), Joie Celis (proof checking), Jon Yamongan (typesetting), and Cleone Baradas (cover design).

ABBREVIATIONS

ADB	Asian Development Bank
ERI	Economic Research Institute
EU	European Union
GDP	gross domestic product
OECD	Organisation for Economic Co-operation and Development
RWI	Regional Well-Being Index
SWI	Subjective Well-Being Index

EXECUTIVE SUMMARY

Kazakhstan is a country where regional inequalities have been growing recently. But regional inequalities are not limited to differences in gross domestic product or income per capita. Regional inequalities—in Kazakhstan and elsewhere—are far broader and encompass differences in access to basic social services and opportunities, and in perceptions. They need to be assessed through holistic tools and comprehensive frameworks that go well beyond pure economic factors and capture subjective well-being, quality of life, and perceptions of opportunities by individuals.

Previous studies of regional inequalities in Kazakhstan have been relatively limited. They have tended to focus on socioeconomic disparities within the country measured by macro-level, objective indicators (for instance, Asian Development Bank [ADB] 2021). This was mainly due to data constraints and the dearth of granular qualitative data at the regional and local levels. These studies have provided valuable information for policymakers. Yet, there is a need to go beyond economic measures of outputs of public services and goods and gather, in addition, evidence on how the provision of public goods and services, as well as quality of life and opportunities, are perceived by households across the country. In other words, data on perceptions of the well-being of population in the regions are essential to have a complete understanding of how and along which lines spatial inequalities in Kazakhstan unfold.

This report analyzes results from the Regional Well-Being Survey of Kazakhstan. This is a novel set of subjective well-being data across all regions (oblasts) in Kazakhstan.

The survey, conducted by the Economic Research Institute between August and November 2022, gathered data on subjective well-being, collected through a countrywide, multidimensional questionnaire. The more than 4,000 responses across all 20 regions in the country unveiled large differences in well-being levels between oblasts. Inhabitants of some oblasts reported subpar levels of satisfaction across dimensions ranging from trust in institutions, satisfaction with financial and housing conditions, quality of health care and education, and perceptions of personal security. For instance, in Almaty region, over 60% of respondents reported that they have difficulties making ends meet, while only around 30% of respondents in East Kazakhstan believe that they are better off than the previous generation.

This report presents two indices constructed using the Regional Well-Being Survey of Kazakhstan: the Subjective Well-Being Index (SWI) and the Regional Well-Being Index (RWI). The objective of both indices is—through the use of only perceptions data in the case of the first index and of both real and perception data in the second index—to shed light on the aggregate performance of oblasts in 10 well-being dimensions, and to inform future policy intervention (map).

Scores of the Regional and the Subjective Well-Being Index

■ First quartile
■ Second quartile
■ Third quartile
□ Fourth quartile

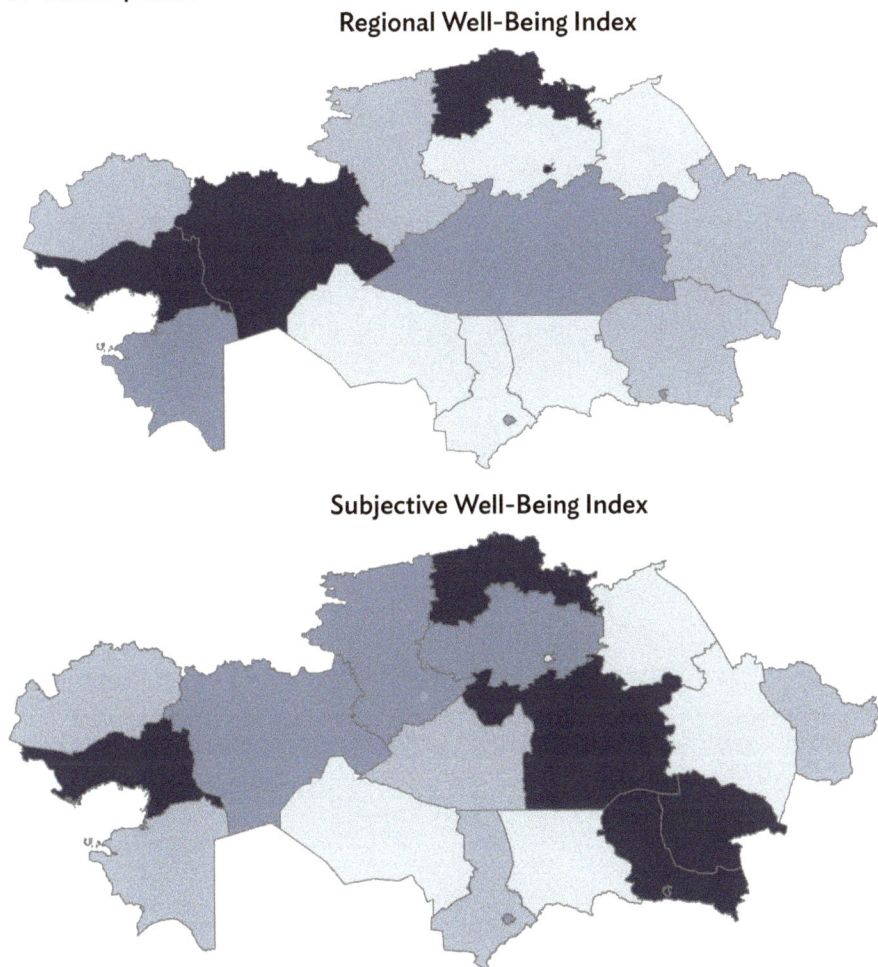

Regional Well-Being Index

Subjective Well-Being Index

Source: Authors.

The SWI is a pure aggregate measure of subjective well-being, while the RWI is a composite index that combines both subjective and objective socioeconomic data. Important insights can be captured by a pillar-by-pillar analysis of the performance of the different oblasts in the country, and by comparing the performance of oblasts across the two indices. For instance, Astana city lies in the top quartile of the distribution of the RWI; however, it falls behind in the SWI. This result points to a low level of satisfaction among residents in Astana, especially when it comes to housing, civic engagement, and social connections. All in all, information on the strengths and weaknesses in socioeconomic well-being of the different oblasts in Kazakhstan can be integrated into policy decisions related to the redistribution of resources from the central to the regional levels of government, to provide equal opportunities that would enable each region to reach its full economic and social potential.

1 INTRODUCTION

Regional inequalities have been a growing issue across both developed and developing countries. The last decades have seen a steady increase in the development of spatially targeted policy interventions aimed at reducing disparities across territories within the same countries. The greater number of policies addressing regional development issues points to the growing importance that spatial inequalities have assumed in the design and implementation of development planning at the national and regional levels. The trend can be observed across a variety of countries. For instance, the Cohesion Fund of the European Union (EU) has been one of the main tools to fight regional inequalities across countries in Europe.[1] Developing economies, such as the People's Republic of China and South Africa, have also implemented policies to combat the growing territorial divides across their regions (Fan et al. 2011, National Planning Commission 2012). The growth of territorial polarization is not just an academic concern, as it can limit both the economic potential of the country and lead to rising discontent which, in turn, can undermine overall economic growth and threaten social and political stability (Iammarino, Rodríguez-Pose, and Storper 2019).

Regional inequalities have also been a growing concern in Kazakhstan. A previous study (ADB 2021) has shown that regional inequalities have been rising rapidly in the country, making already large gaps in wealth, economic dynamism, and competitiveness even larger. The study has also shown that, while gross domestic product (GDP) per capita has increased in Kazakhstan over the past 20 years, the additional wealth linked to this economic growth has been concentrated in a limited number of regions. In other territories, the recent economic gains deriving from Kazakhstan's economic dynamism and integration in international markets have been limited. These inequalities, in turn, carry non-negligible opportunity costs and risk fueling social tensions and unrest. Indeed, the presence of lagging-behind regions represents a huge source of untapped socioeconomic development potential. At the same time, there is evidence to suggest that spatial inequalities may lead to rising discontent and anti-establishment sentiments, which can quickly unravel and lead to significant unrest (Rodriguez-Pose 2018).

Although there have been attempts to understand the pattern of regional inequalities across Kazakhstan, previous studies largely focused on input and/or output macro-level measures. For instance, ADB has assessed regional economies across six dimensions such as labor conditions,

---

[1] Cohesion policy is the EU's investment program to help regional development. It aims to reduce economic, social, and territorial disparities between EU regions, channeling investment through three main funds: the European Regional Development Fund, the European Social Fund, and the Cohesion Fund. Through the Cohesion Fund, the EU funds development policies in lagging-behind regions and its investments help to deliver many EU policy objectives and complement EU policies such as those dealing with employment, energy, the environment, the single market, research and innovation, education, and culture (European Commission 2013).

education, and health (ADB 2021). The variables of choice, however, were confined to input and output measures such as the number of universities, infant mortality, and employment rate. As discussed throughout this report, while these variables are usually the most accessible ones across national and regional statistical offices, they do not represent the full picture of inequalities in Kazakhstan. Inefficiencies in the provision of public services often determine variations in outcomes across regions of the same country. Hence, regions with the same number of universities, for example, may exhibit different levels of satisfaction across their population.

Incorporating more perception-laden and outcome-based variables in the assessment of regional economies and societies can provide a far fuller and more realistic picture while complementing the more traditional approach based on hard economic and endowment measures. In this regard, the concept of well-being can be useful to provide a solid conceptual framework. While well-being has only recently started to inform policymaking and regional development policies, there are several guidelines and best practices that can be singled out for the development of well-being measures across regions and countries (for instance, Organisation for Economic Co-operation and Development [OECD] 2011). In this report, we develop both the methodology and the empirics of two complementary Well-Being indices that can be applied to measure well-being across Kazakhstan's regions. The proposed indices build on a comprehensive literature review of best practices on both the measurement of well-being through survey data, such as the European Social Survey, the World Values Survey, and the European Values Survey, and the computation of well-being indices, such as the OECD Better Life Index. The indices are designed to allow policymakers to develop a better understanding of certain well-being phenomena, which are not necessarily captured by the more traditional indicators such as GDP, productivity, employment, or inequality. A prime example is the study of well-being levels in Arab countries immediately prior to the so-called Arab Spring in 2011—while the main economic indicators, like GDP per capita, reflected a picture of increased wealth and surging incomes across many Arab countries, subjective well-being measures clearly pointed to a fast downward trend in the years immediately prior to the social revolts (Gallup 2011).

Furthermore, the current system of regional standards widely used across Kazakhstan to assess living standards in each oblast could be considered outdated. More importantly, it fails to capture significant nuances of well-being outcomes. As the current system largely relies on output measures, such as the minimum number of schools or hospitals that need to be present in a certain territory to ensure comparable standards across all regions, outcome measures are mostly, if not totally, neglected. For this reason, the current study and methodology assumes a timely importance to contribute to develop the policy frameworks and tools used to inform the decisions of policymakers.

Thanks to the collection—by the Economic Research Institute (ERI) of Kazakhstan and the behest of ADB—an analysis of a novel set of primary data, the findings stemming from this report not only confirm the highly spatially uneven picture presented by previous studies (ADB 2021), but also add significant qualitative detail on the underlying characteristics of such regional imbalances. The scenario depicted by the two indices developed in this study—the Subjective Well-Being Index (SWI) and the Regional Well-Being Index (RWI)—exposes the higher levels of well-being of city regions and western and northern oblasts relative to the rest of the country. That said, once a pillar-by-pillar analysis is carried out, weaknesses emerge in even the stronger oblasts. Similarly, weaker oblasts, such as those in the east and south of the country, can also have higher scores when other well-being indicators, such as personal safety or social connections, are considered. This points to the importance of acknowledging the underlying differences among regions to design and implement informed policy actions that target region-specific bottlenecks.

2 THE REGIONAL WELL-BEING SURVEY OF KAZAKHSTAN: BUILDING A SUBJECTIVE WELL-BEING INDEX

2.1 Defining Well-Being and Why It Matters

The measurement of well-being at a regional level in Kazakhstan is a relatively new endeavor for researchers and policymakers alike. Across the world, the concept of well-being has only recently become popular among researchers and policymakers alike. Measuring well-being is part of the global effort to overcome hard economic indicators, such as GDP or gross national income, as the dominant measures of prosperity and development. Given the relative novelty of the concept both worldwide and in Kazakhstan, in the next paragraphs we set the theoretical and conceptual bases for the empirical work that is to follow. This puts the foundation for the collection of data on subjective well-being across Kazakhstan's oblasts.

There are at least three good reasons to measure well-being and dedicate resources in evaluating it. First, measures of well-being can complement other outcome measures. With reference to policymakers, measuring well-being can be helpful and valuable as an indicator of progress when it can alert policymakers to issues that other, more conventional social and economic indicators may fail to detect. This important, complementary role of well-being measures is reinforced by events of the last decade, such as the insurrections that took place across several Arab countries at the beginning of the 2010s—the so-called Arab Spring. Both Tunisia and Egypt experienced a rise in GDP per capita levels in the years immediately before the breakout of revolts, with Egyptian GDP per capita growing at around 34% in real terms between 2005 and 2010 (International Monetary Fund 2022).[2] However, when looking at the trajectory of life satisfaction in the two countries, a downward trend was evident. During the same period, the proportion of Tunisians reporting high levels of well-being fell from 24% to 14%. In Egypt, the drop was even steeper, from 29% to 12% (Gallup 2011). The evidence stemming from the trajectories in terms of well-being in the two Arab countries is illustrative of the type of relevance that data on well-being can assume. In other words, well-being measures can shed light on underlying social issues which would otherwise be overlooked by conventional indicators such as GDP growth, employment, or productivity.

A second major use of measures of well-being is to help identify what factors are critical for people's well-being. This use of well-being measures can be particularly useful when attempting to capture progress, testing whether the outcomes used to measure progress align with the factors that shape people's perceptions of their life satisfaction (Halpern 2010). Relatedly, measures of well-being help understand the trade-offs between different outcomes and generally, what people are more concerned about. Third and finally, measuring well-being is useful when evaluating the impact and outcomes

---

[2]   Data on GDP per capita were retrieved from the International Monetary Fund's World Economic Outlook Database.

of specific social and economic policies. A prime example of how this can be done is represented by the Green Book, the formal guidance from the Treasury of the United Kingdom (UK) to other UK government agencies on how to appraise and evaluate policy proposals. In 2011, the Green Book and its valuation techniques for social cost–benefit analysis were updated to include measures of life satisfaction alongside the more conventional approaches adopted in cost–benefit analysis (Fujiwara and Campbell 2011). In this regard, measures of well-being can be used either prior to policy implementation and design, or in their aftermath, as a way to determine whether the intended policy outcome has been achieved.

Defining the concept of well-being is crucial to ensure the relevance and accuracy of survey questions. In this study, we use the OECD's definition of well-being as "the good mental states, including all of the various evaluations, positive and negative, that people make of their lives, and the affective reactions of people to their experiences" (OECD 2013, p.10). The definition largely builds on the theoretical work carried out by the OECD and its Better Life Index. It also closely reflects Diener's (2006, p. 400) subjective well-being, for whom "well-being is an umbrella term for the different valuations people make regarding their lives, the events happening to them, their bodies and minds, and the circumstances in which they live." Moreover, for the collection of survey data, we focus on three key aspects of well-being: (i) life evaluations, (ii) affection, and (iii) psychological flourishing or eudaimonic well-being (Kahneman and Krueger 2006, Helliwell and Barrington-Leigh 2010, Clark and Senik 2010).[3] This means that the survey questions included in the Regional Well-Being Survey of Kazakhstan collect data on cognitive and reflective assessments of a person's life or some specific domains of it—for instance, while it is possible to measure "life as a whole" through global judgments, it is also possible for people to provide evaluations of particular aspects of their lives like health or their job (Helliwell and Barrington-Leigh 2010). It also includes measures of affection that aim to assess specific feelings or emotional states with reference to the present. Finally, when it comes to psychological flourishing, we focus on the more "functioning" aspect of well-being, which includes capturing autonomy, competence, interest in learning, goal orientation, sense of purpose, resilience, and social engagement (Huppert 2009).

2.2   Survey Specification

The Regional Well-Being Survey of Kazakhstan collected data between August and November 2022. The data were collected by a team of researchers at the ERI of Kazakhstan. This is consistent with international best practice, such as the European Social Survey, which indicates that data should be collected over a period no less than 5 months. The collection of data was aimed at ensuring a fair representation across Kazakhstan's oblasts. A total of 4,034 individual surveys were conducted, following a preestablished questionnaire based on best practices such as the World Values Survey, the European Social Survey, and the European Values Survey. The distribution of observations across each oblast is reported in Table 1. The survey adopts the new territorial classification of oblasts implemented by the Government of Kazakhstan in 2022. This includes the three new oblasts of Abay, Ulytau, and Zhetysu.

---

[3]   Eudaimonic well-being refers to quality of life derived from the development of a person's best potentials and their application in the fulfillment of personally expressive, self-concordant goals (Ryan and Deci 2001).

Table 1: Sample Sizes by Kazakhstan's Oblasts

Oblast	Population ('000)	Share of Population (%)	Sample Size
Abay	610.2	3	167
Akmola	786.7	4	164
Aktobe	925.9	5	183
Almaty region	1,499.8	8	235
Atyrau	690.8	4	161
West Kazakhstan	687.0	3	163
Zhambyl	1,216.2	6	205
Karaganda	1,134.3	6	180
Kostanay	832.3	4	199
Kyzylorda	831.7	4	161
Mangystau	763.2	4	165
Pavlodar	754.8	4	179
North Kazakhstan	534.7	3	164
Turkestan	2,113.4	11	338
East Kazakhstan	730.6	4	165
Astana city	1,340.8	7	238
Almaty city	2,151.8	1	425
Shymkent city	1,186.5	6	222
Ulytau	221.2	1	166
Zhetysu	698.7	4	161

Sources: Government of Kazakhstan, Bureau of National Statistics, Authors.

The questionnaire of the survey is in Annex 1. Data were collected through personal interviews, meaning that the interviewer was personally present when recording the responses. Among the literature, personal interviews are often considered a fair compromise between telephone interviews, which are usually regarded as the least reliable option for collecting consistent data on well-being, and self-reported interviews—that is when the respondents enter their own data into a computer-generated or online questionnaire—often not guaranteeing representativeness and reducing the risk of socially desirable responding (OECD 2013).[4] The target population included individuals aged 18 or older (with no upper age limit) residing in any given region within private households at the date of beginning of fieldwork. This practice is in line with other internationally renowned surveys such as the World Values Survey and the European Social Survey.

---

[4]   Socially desirable responding is typically defined as the tendency to give positive self-descriptions.

Based on the theoretical understandings on what affects well-being, the team introduced the following 10 domains, organized under three headline categories:

(i) Subjective well-being:
    (a) life satisfaction.

(ii) Material conditions:
    (a) income,
    (b) jobs, and
    (c) housing conditions.

(iii) Quality of life:
    (a) social capital, civic engagement, and governance;
    (b) infrastructure;
    (c) social connections and work–life balance;
    (d) health and education;
    (e) environment and natural capital; and
    (f) personal security.

Income and wealth capture people's current and future consumption possibilities. Both the availability of jobs and their quality are relevant for material well-being, not only because they increase the number of resources available to people, but also because of the role of personal fulfillment and self-esteem that a job can grant individuals. Housing and its quality are crucial to meet basic needs and have a sense of personal security, privacy, and personal space (Oswald et al. 2003, OECD 2011). Health status is important, but it is also important to perform a range of activities related to well-being, such as work (Dolan, Peasgood, and White 2008). Similarly, education is a great asset for raising living standards, but it is also an aspiration by many people. Work–life balance contributes to well-being as it measures the ability of spending time on non-remunerated activities that help people remain healthy and productive (Helliwell 2008, OECD 2013). Civic engagement and quality of governance matters for well-being, as it allows people to have more control over their lives (Helliwell and Wang 2011). Social connectedness helps fulfill many personal goals, and the quality of the environment also shapes personal health and well-being (Dolan, Peasgood, and White 2008; Boarini et al. 2012). Finally, considering people's feelings and evaluations indicates the degree of overall satisfaction of individual citizens (OECD 2013).

During the post-survey phase, the data collected were carefully coded and cleaned. The data-cleaning procedures included checking for duplicate records, loss of records, incomplete responses, out-of-range responses, among other errors. When dealing with subjective and qualitative measures, researchers must look for response sets, that is, when respondents provide identical ratings on numerical scales to a series of different items. For instance, this can happen when a respondent answers identically across questions across whole modules. This suggests that respondents are not responding meaningfully; hence, we treat such responses as non-response and discard them. The number of such responses was, however, minimal fundamentally as a result of the survey being conducted in person by trained personnel of ERI.

2.3   The Methodology for the Subjective Well-Being Index

Using the collected and cleaned-up dataset, we proceeded to construct an index purely based on the survey results: the Subjective Well-Being Index (SWI) for Kazakhstan. The computation of aggregate indices had been advocated in the past as a source of easily accessible and comparable data on well-being (for example, refer to Stiglitz and Fitoussi 2009 for a review). The main objective of such an index is to assess the local and regional perceptions of residents on their living conditions and well-being standards, but also on the quality of the public goods and services provided to them and the life opportunities they have wherever they live in Kazakhstan. Compared with other sources of well-being data, the SWI captures exclusively public services outcomes, rather than outputs of, for example, the regional education and health-care systems and labor markets. This is also a main factor of differentiation compared with other indices of regional inequality in Kazakhstan developed in the past, such as the Regional Competitiveness and Cohesion Index, which mostly reflected outputs and inputs of public spending. In this sense, the SWI—and, to a lesser extent, the Regional Well-Being Index (RWI) that follows—can infer not only on the overall state of well-being, but also detect inefficiencies in, for instance, the education and/or health systems across regions. In the case of two regions with similar levels of inputs in, for example, health expenditure but significantly divergent satisfaction levels, this could point to a more (or less) efficient use of public money across those two regions.

When it comes to the computation technique, the SWI follows best practice. The index is built on the three headline categories identified for the collection of data through the survey—subjective well-being, material conditions, and quality of life. Each category includes 10 sub-dimensions, or domains (for a full specification, refer to the previous section). The computation consists of a step-by-step aggregation process. For this study, we choose simple aggregation methods. This implies the use of arithmetic means to calculate the scores of each dimension. First, the individual indicators are normalized using the z-score normalization formula:

$$\frac{value - \mu}{\sigma}$$

Each dimension is calculated as the simple arithmetic mean of a region's performance in the indicators selected. The scores for the 10 sub-dimensions are computed as arithmetic means of the dimension scores. The choice of the simple arithmetic mean helps keep the index as simple as possible with the data gathered. It also makes it relatively straightforward to replicate. This construction of the index allows for certain dimensions to enter the index with a negative sign, such as perceived corruption. Finally, the last step consists of computing the SWI as an average of all dimensions. This process was repeated for all oblasts in Kazakhstan to have comparable scores. Following best practice, no specific weights were assigned to individual indicators or dimensions, implying that all indicators were treated as equally important in the index.

One fundamental advantage of the SWI is the possibility to compile aggregate information for each oblast and list each region according to a ranking of well-being. This provides a relatively straightforward way for policymakers to detect critical areas for improvement in each territory. Indeed, whereas the ranking of oblasts based on the overall score of the SWI depicts the general picture, rankings along each dimension of well-being can help identify the "weaker links" in each oblast. Although certain oblasts may exhibit high levels of overall well-being, they might be below average in specific dimensions.

2.4   Findings

Overall Scores

The ranking and scores of the SWI are illustrated in Table 2 according to quartiles of the distribution. The oblasts of Zhetysu and Karaganda top the ranking, with scores that clearly stand out from the rest of the distribution. These two oblasts display high levels of reported well-being. Also, in the first quartile but at considerable distance, we find North Kazakhstan, Almaty region, and Atyrau. These three oblasts show levels of well-being still significantly above the country's average. These oblasts make the top quartile in terms of overall subjective well-being. They include both high-income regions, such as Atyrau, and more rural regions. The second quartile encompasses two city regions, Almaty city and Shymkent city, together with Aktobe, Kostanay, and Akmola. Finally, the third and fourth quartiles of the distribution include mostly central and southern regions comprising Ulytau, Abay, Kyzylorda, and Zhambyl. Astana also appears in the bottom half of the ranking, indicating lower-than-average levels of well-being in the capital of Kazakhstan.

Table 2: Ranking and Scores of the Subjective Well-Being Index for Kazakhstan

Rank	Oblast	Subjective Well-Being Index
1	Zhetysu	1.07
2	Karaganda	0.94
3	North Kazakhstan	0.82
4	Atyrau	0.76
5	Almaty region	0.42
6	Almaty city	0.40
7	Aktobe	0.37
8	Shymkent city	0.27
9	Kostanay	0.17
10	Akmola	0.09
11	Mangystau	0.03
12	West Kazakhstan	(0.11)
13	East Kazakhstan	(0.21)
14	Ulytau	(0.38)
15	Turkestan	(0.39)
16	Astana city	(0.41)
17	Abay	(0.63)
18	Kyzylorda	(0.93)
19	Pavlodar	(1.10)
20	Zhambyl	(1.18)

Note: Highlighted from dark green to red are regions according to quartiles of the distribution (e.g., regions highlighted in dark green are in the top quartile).

Source: Authors.

Map 1 helps visualize the distribution across the 20 oblasts of Kazakhstan. The regions that display the highest levels of reported subjective well-being are located in the west and north of Kazakhstan. Interestingly, Zhetysu, Almaty region, Karaganda, and Almaty city display higher well-being levels compared with neighboring regions both in the east and south of the country. In any case, except for the territory once covered by the sole oblast of Almaty and now divided into Zhetysu and Almaty, and the region of Karaganda, those living in western and northern regions tend to display higher levels of life satisfaction. To better understand the differences across oblasts in each of the three macro-dimensions, the next three subsections look at the performance of individual oblasts according to the categorization of the SWI.

Map 1: Subjective Well-Being Index of Kazakhstan, by Oblast

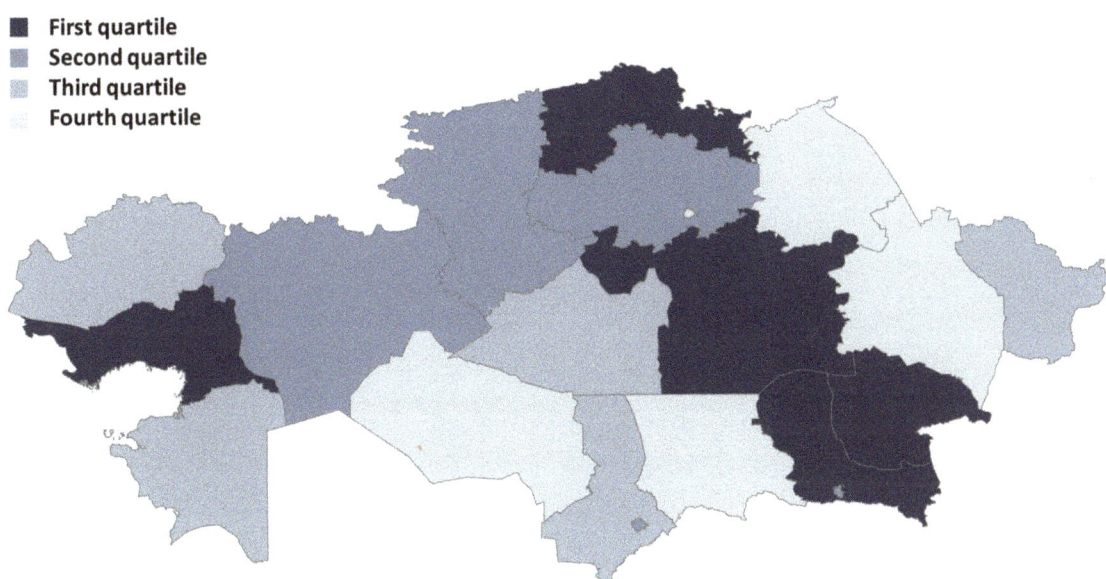

Source: Authors.

Almaty city and Shymkent city exhibit higher or similar scores on the index compared with their neighboring regions, Almaty region and Turkestan. In contrast, Astana city performs poorly in the index, with its score significantly lower than that of neighboring region of Akmola. To better understand the characteristics of the city regions of Kazakhstan, Figure 1 illustrates the performance of the cities in each of the sub-dimension of the index. As we can observe, there are non-negligible differences across the three cities. Overall, households in Astana city report the lowest satisfaction levels, with only responses related to personal security being higher than both Almaty city and Shymkent city. Additionally, Astana city seems to perform relatively poorly when it comes to satisfaction with social connections and work–life balance, and health and education services. In contrast, Almaty city displays the highest levels of subjective well-being, measured as life satisfaction and meaning, material conditions, and health and education. However, Almaty city has relatively low scores when it comes to social connections and work–life balance, and it has the lowest score among the three cities in social capital and governance. This may indicate residents' lower trust in the local government, together with stronger perceptions of corruption. Finally, Shymkent city performs well in the dimensions of social capital and social connections and work–life balance, while it is generally perceived as less safe and poorer than Astana city and Almaty city. This is reflected in lower scores in dimensions such as personal security and material conditions.

Figure 1: Performance of Cities in the Subjective Well-Being Index, by Dimension

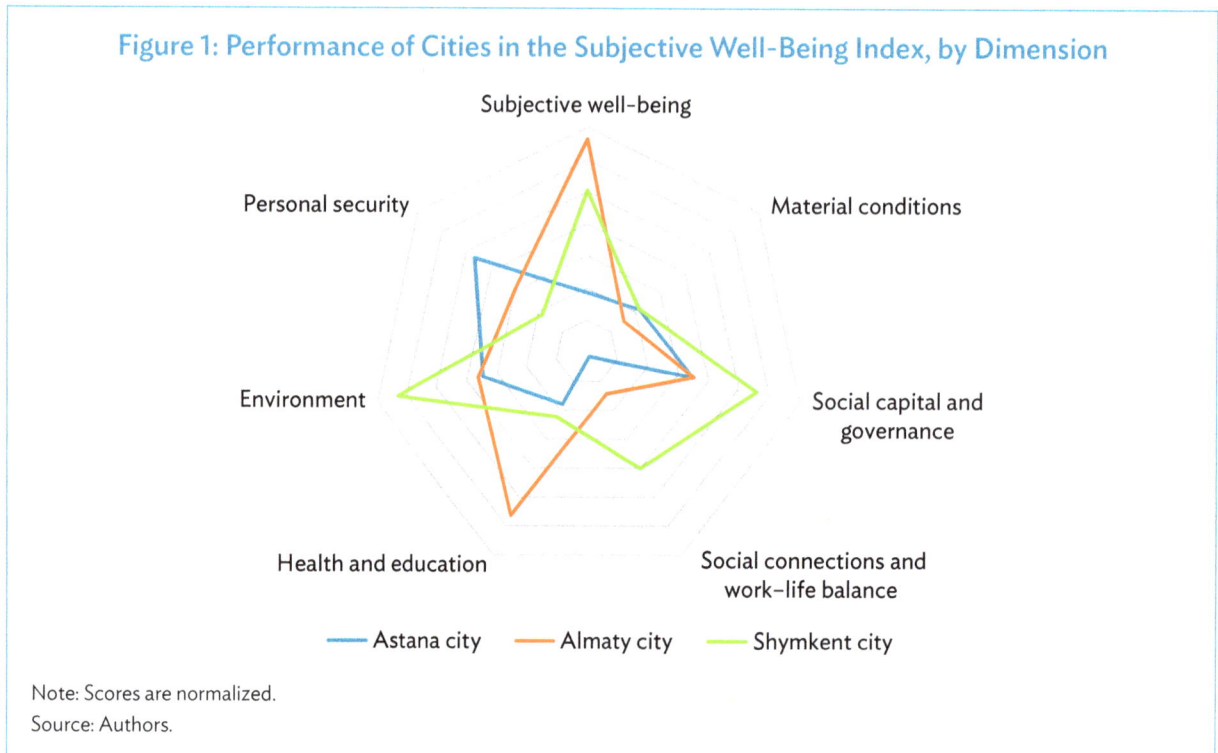

Note: Scores are normalized.
Source: Authors.

Material Conditions

In the SWI, material conditions refer to respondents' perceptions and satisfaction around topics such as income, job quality, and housing conditions. In this sense, households reporting lower scores in this dimension might have difficulties making ends meet, or they are unsatisfied with the local labor markets and housing options. Table 3 illustrates the ranking of Kazakhstan's oblasts according to their normalized scores in the "material conditions" headline dimension. Again, Karaganda tops the ranking. Map 2 helps visualize which oblasts display better scores in the material conditions dimension. At the top of the ranking, we find many northern and western oblasts such as North Kazakhstan, Atyrau, Akmola, Aktobe, and West Kazakhstan. This group of regions is joined by Karaganda and Zhetysu. Eastern and southern oblasts, in contrast, tend to show lower scores.

Table 3: Ranking of Kazakhstan's Oblasts on Material Conditions, per Individual Scores

Rank	Oblast	Normalized Score
1	Karaganda	2.23
2	North Kazakhstan	1.71
3	Zhetysu	1.46
4	Atyrau	0.91
5	Aktobe	0.61
6	Kostanay	0.57
7	Almaty region	0.17
8	Akmola	0.05
9	West Kazakhstan	0.05
10	Ulytau	(0.06)
11	Mangystau	(0.06)
12	Shymkent city	(0.43)
13	Astana city	(0.43)
14	East Kazakhstan	(0.64)
15	Almaty city	(0.73)
16	Abay	(0.85)
17	Turkestan	(0.99)
18	Kyzylorda	(1.01)
19	Pavlodar	(1.07)
20	Zhambyl	(1.48)

( ) = negative

Note: Highlighted from dark green to red are regions according to quartiles of the distribution (e.g., regions highlighted in dark green are in the top quartile).

Source: Authors.

Map 2: Representation of Normalized Scores on Material Conditions, by Oblast

- First quartile
- Second quartile
- Third quartile
- Fourth quartile

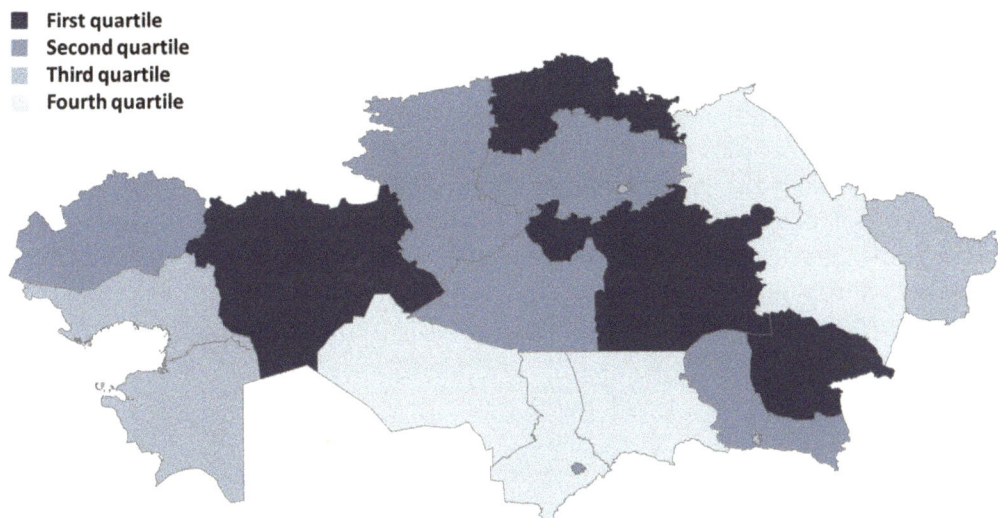

Source: Authors.

An important aspect within material conditions is households' financial and economic stability. Figure 2 shows the percentage of people who reported having difficulties in making ends meet across Kazakhstan's oblasts. On average, across the country, 51% of households report having difficulties making ends meet. This percentage reaches over 60% in Almaty region. Many regions in the east and west display higher than average percentages. In Zhetysu, Almaty city, Ulytau, East Kazakhstan, and Turkestan, between 54% and 62% of respondents are in dire and unstable economic circumstances.

Figure 2: Percentage of Respondents Having Difficulties Making Ends Meet

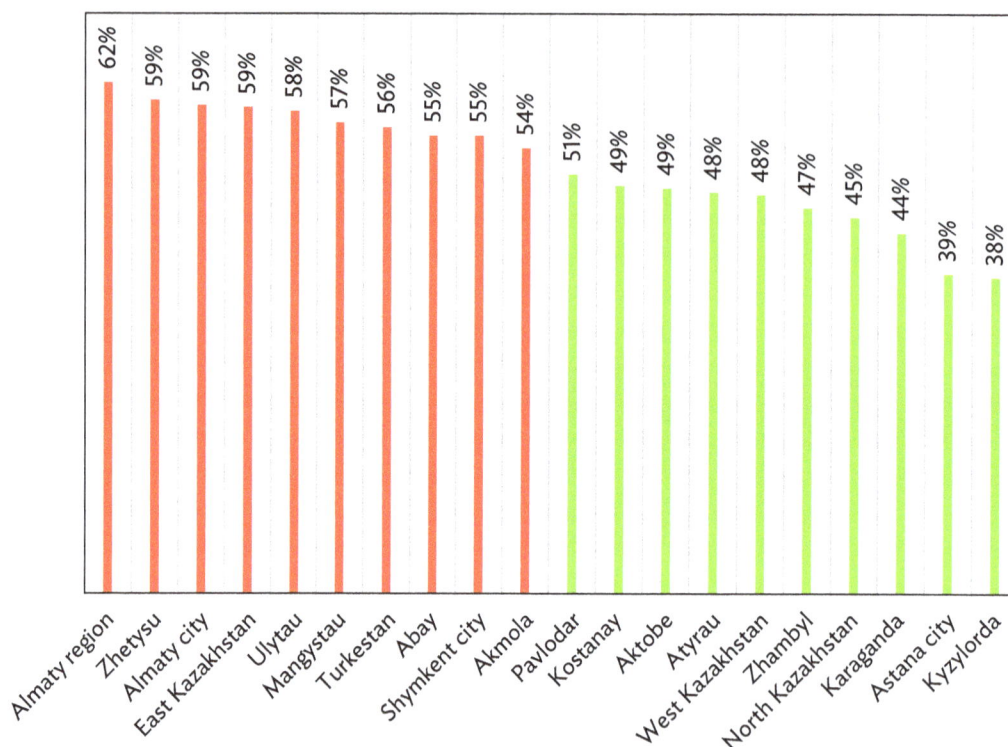

Housing conditions and satisfaction also vary across Kazakhstan (Figure 3). In Zhetysu, 87% of respondents claim they are satisfied with their housing conditions. Most regions in the north and west of the country are above the country average, that is, 78% of respondents report being satisfied with their housing conditions. In contrast, regions such as Turkestan, Kyzylorda, Abay, Pavlodar, and Zhambyl all fall below the country average. The cities of Almaty, Shymkent, and Astana perform worse than the rest, with Almaty city and Astana city being at the bottom of the distribution. This may indicate the need for better and more inclusive urban housing plans in the largest cities of the country, to improve the living and housing conditions of residents, especially those in the lowest ends of the income distribution.

Figure 3: Percentage of Respondents Satisfied with Their Housing Conditions

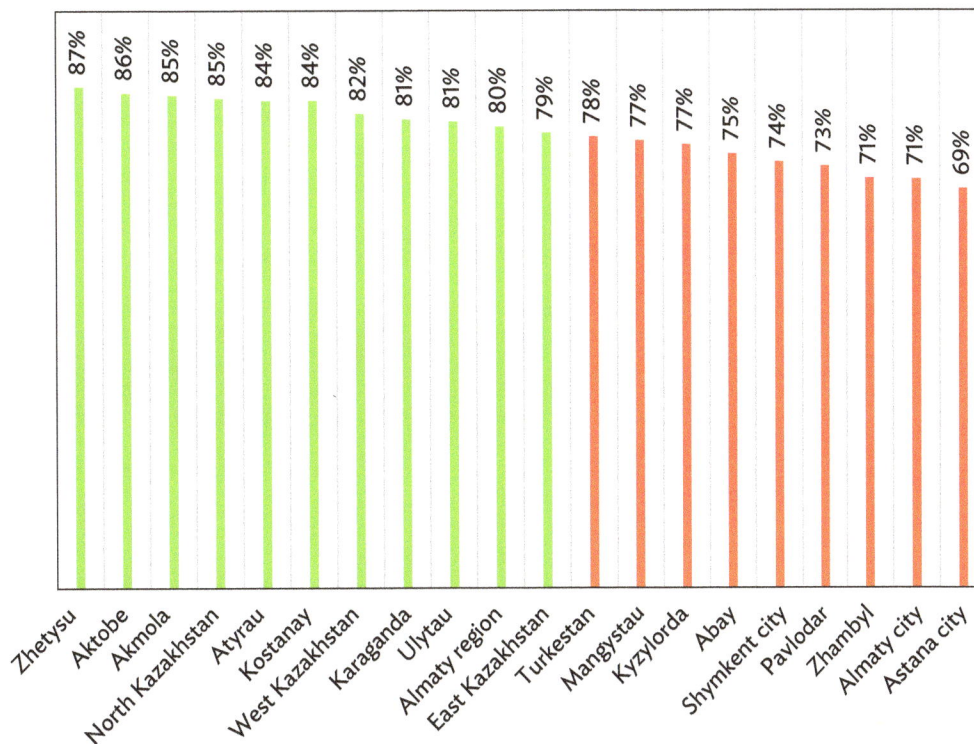

Region	%
Zhetysu	87%
Aktobe	86%
Akmola	85%
North Kazakhstan	85%
Atyrau	84%
Kostanay	84%
West Kazakhstan	82%
Karaganda	81%
Ulytau	81%
Almaty region	80%
East Kazakhstan	79%
Turkestan	78%
Mangystau	77%
Kyzylorda	77%
Abay	75%
Shymkent city	74%
Pavlodar	73%
Zhambyl	71%
Almaty city	71%
Astana city	69%

Source: Authors.

Finally, it is worth looking at respondents' perceptions when asked whether they felt they were better off, worse off, or about the same compared with their parents' living standards. This question, although highly subjective, may point to discontent among the local population when it comes to economic opportunities and, in general, intergenerational social mobility. Figure 4 shows the percentages across each oblast. In many oblasts, less than 50% of respondents believe that their living conditions are any better than those of their parents. There is also great variation across oblasts. In Karaganda, 62% of the sample population report being better off than their parents, and in East Kazakhstan and Turkestan, it is a mere 33%. The sense of little or no improvement in intergenerational living conditions affects oblasts across the board both in the east and in the west. That said, eastern and southern regions tend to be below the country average, with oblasts such as East Kazakhstan, Turkestan, Shymkent city, Abay, and Zhetysu where less than 40% of respondents report better living standards than their parents. While this data may seem in direct contradiction with data stemming from GDP per capita growth over the past 2 decades (Map 3), socioeconomic trends, such as an increased spatial polarization of wealth in certain areas of the country, may have contributed to lower local perceptions on wealth and economic opportunities.

Figure 4: Percentage of Respondents Who Reported Having Better Living Standards Than Their Parents

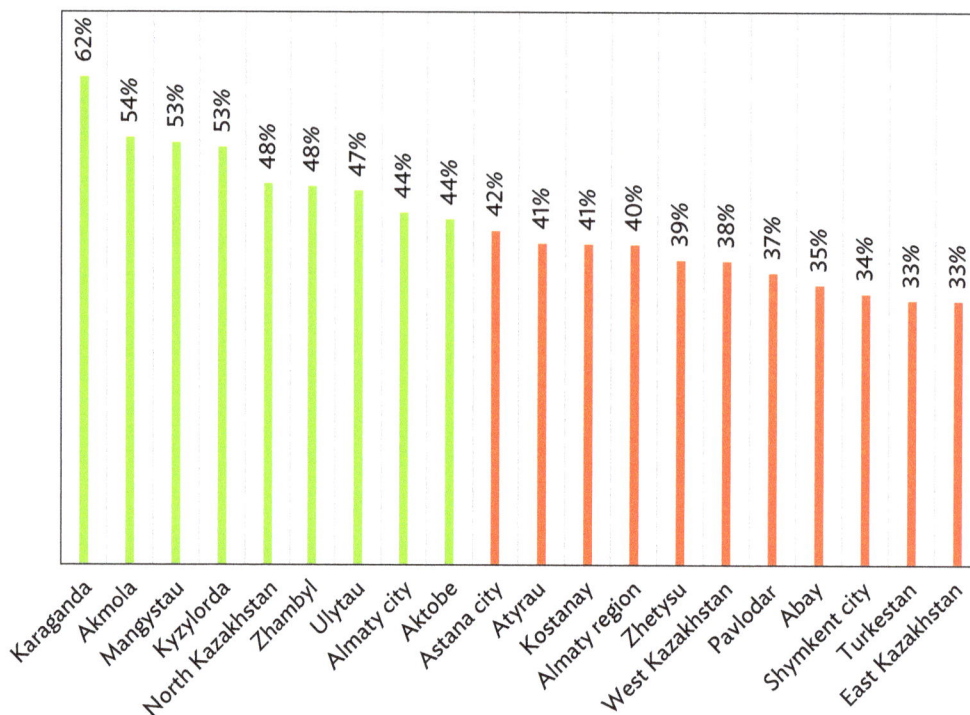

Source: Authors.

Map 3: Comparison between Material Conditions of the Subjective Well-Being Index and Gross Domestic Product per Capita

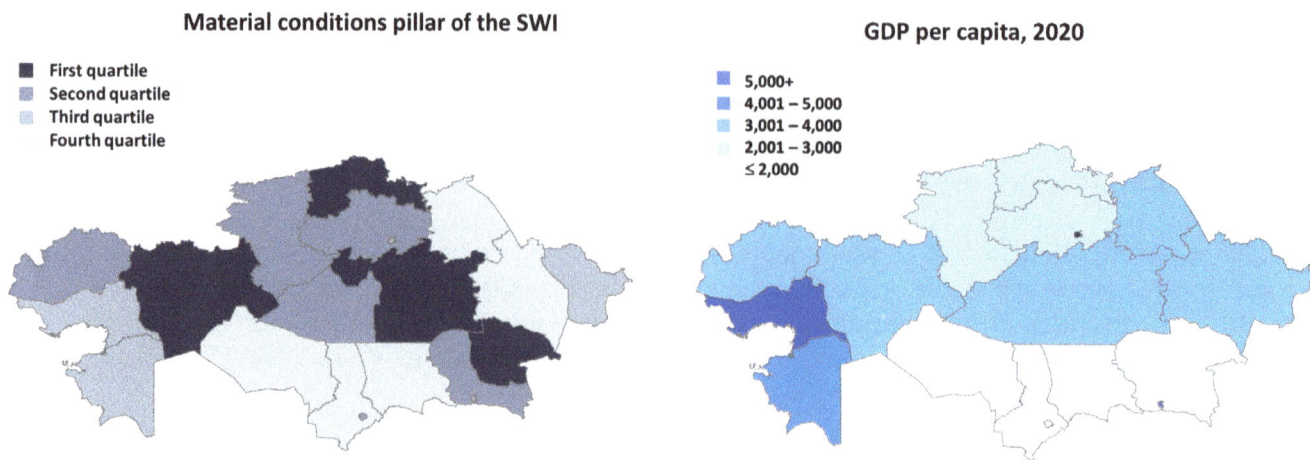

Material conditions pillar of the SWI

- First quartile
- Second quartile
- Third quartile
- Fourth quartile

GDP per capita, 2020

- 5,000+
- 4,001 – 5,000
- 3,001 – 4,000
- 2,001 – 3,000
- ≤ 2,000

GDP = gross domestic product. SWI = Subject Well-Being Index.
Source: Authors.

Quality of Life

The second pillar of the SWI is defined as quality of life, and it encompasses a variety of subdimensions, including social capital and governance, infrastructure social connections, health and education, natural capital, and personal security. This pillar aims to capture the more indirect factors that affect individual perceptions of well-being. Table 4 illustrates the ranking of Kazakhstan's oblasts according to normalized scores of quality of life, while Map 4 plots the scores on the map. Values are computed by aggregating scores under each subdimension, as detailed in the methodology part of this report. The results show North Kazakhstan, Zhetysu, Akmola, West Kazakhstan, and Shymkent city at the top of the ranking, while a diverse group of oblasts (comprising northern, eastern, and central regions) falls at the bottom of the ranking. Interestingly, Astana city is the worst performing among the three cities, and its score comes after that of some lagging-behind oblasts such as Turkestan or East Kazakhstan.

Table 4: Ranking of Oblasts on Quality of Life

Rank	Oblast	Normalized Score
1	North Kazakhstan	1.29
2	Zhetysu	1.27
3	Akmola	0.42
4	West Kazakhstan	0.26
5	Shymkent city	0.23
6	Atyrau	0.14
7	Almaty city	0.11
8	Almaty region	0.09
9	Aktobe	0.03
10	Turkestan	0.02
11	Mangystau	(0.01)
12	Kyzylorda	(0.20)
13	East Kazakhstan	(0.21)
14	Astana city	(0.24)
15	Zhambyl	(0.31)
16	Pavlodar	(0.32)
17	Karaganda	(0.37)
18	Abay	(0.55)
19	Kostanay	(0.58)
20	Ulytau	(1.05)

( ) = negative.

Note: Highlighted from dark green to red are regions according to quartiles of the distribution (e.g., regions highlighted in dark green are in the top quartile).

Source: Authors.

Map 4: Representation of Normalized Scores on Quality of Life, by Oblast

- First quartile
- Second quartile
- Third quartile
- Fourth quartile

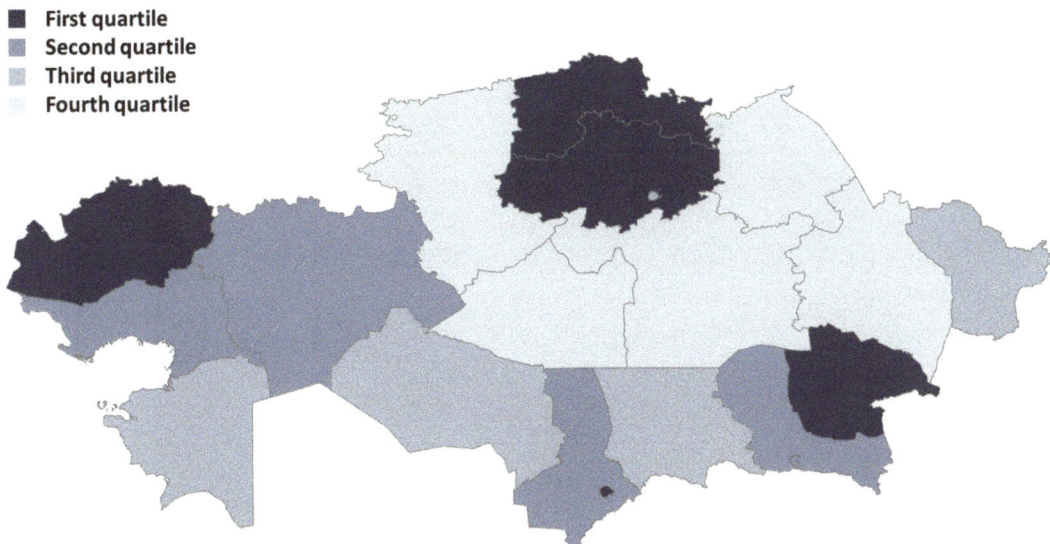

Source: Authors.

While the headline dimension quality of life can be a useful aggregate measure of well-being related to a diverse set of topics, an analysis of each oblast's performance in the underlying sub-dimensions can shed light on the strengths and weaknesses of the 20 regions of Kazakhstan. Table 5 summarizes the performance of each oblast in all six sub-dimensions of the quality of life pillar. Although several regions tend to consistently outperform others, even regions with high scores display lower scores in individual dimensions. For instance, while North Kazakhstan's scores tend to fall in the top quartile of the distribution across all six dimensions, its score under infrastructure reflects an average performance. Similarly, East Kazakhstan's scores are in the bottom half of the table under almost all dimensions. That said, respondents seem relatively satisfied with the quality of the local governance and with security standards and law enforcement. At least two other factors are worth noting. First, we can observe how the ranking is relatively unrelated to each region's GDP per capita levels. If we take, for instance, the oil-rich region of Atyrau, we see that its performance is below average in three out of six dimensions—social capital, health and education, and environment and natural capital. The region tops the ranking only under social connections and work–life balance, while it has average scores when it comes to infrastructure. Such a performance reiterates the importance of collecting this type of granular data as compared with widely available data such as GDP. In addition, a diverse regional performance points to those areas of a person's life that, with time, could fuel discontent in any given region. In this sense, discontent in each region may be driven by slightly different causes, may it be poor infrastructure, the lack of adequate health care and education, or perceived corruption and lack of trust in the local governance.

Table 5: Summary of Oblasts' Performance in Quality of Life Subdimensions

Social Capital and Governance	Infrastructure	Social Connections	Health and Education	Environment	Personal Security
Zhetysu	Shymkent city	Atyrau	Kyzylorda	Zhetysu	North Kazakhstan
Shymkent city	Astana city	Turkestan	North Kazakhstan	Almaty region	Karaganda
North Kazakhstan	Almaty city	Kyzylorda	Almaty city	West Kazakhstan	Aktobe
East Kazakhstan	Pavlodar	Aktobe	Zhambyl	Akmola	Akmola
Almaty region	Zhetysu	Zhetysu	Zhetysu	North Kazakhstan	Astana city
Pavlodar	Mangystau	Shymkent city	West Kazakhstan	Zhambyl	Atyrau
Almaty city	Almaty region	West Kazakhstan	Akmola	Turkestan	Zhetysu
Astana city	Turkestan	North Kazakhstan	Karaganda	Shymkent city	East Kazakhstan
Abay	Atyrau	Mangystau	Aktobe	Mangystau	Abay
Kostanay	Zhambyl	Akmola	Almaty region	East Kazakhstan	Almaty city
Mangystau	North Kazakhstan	Almaty region	Atyrau	Pavlodar	Pavlodar
Turkestan	Kyzylorda	East Kazakhstan	Shymkent city	Almaty city	West Kazakhstan
Ulytau	West Kazakhstan	Karaganda	Mangystau	Astana city	Mangystau
Akmola	Akmola	Zhambyl	Abay	Aktobe	Shymkent city
West Kazakhstan	Ulytau	Almaty city	Turkestan	Kostanay	Kyzylorda
Karaganda	Karaganda	Kostanay	Pavlodar	Atyrau	Kostanay
Atyrau	Kostanay	Ulytau	Astana city	Abay	Zhambyl
Aktobe	East Kazakhstan	Pavlodar	Kostanay	Ulytau	Turkestan
Kyzylorda	Aktobe	Astana city	Ulytau	Kyzylorda	Almaty region
Zhambyl	Abay	Abay	East Kazakhstan	Karaganda	Ulytau

Source: Authors.

Second, it is worth observing the performance of some lagging-behind regions, as identified by previous studies through the computation of convergence indices (see, for instance, ADB 2021). Turkestan, for example, lies around the country average in the overall quality of life score; however, its scores vary quite significantly across each dimension. Turkestan's best performance can be observed in social connections and work–life balance, natural capital, and infrastructure. In contrast, the oblast performs below average in social capital, health and education, and the personal security dimension (Figure 5 shows the perceptions on health care in Turkestan). The identification of such strengths and weaknesses can inform future policy actions aimed at improving socioeconomic living conditions in the region, while also tackling pockets of local discontent among its population. For instance, large infrastructural investments in the form of new roads, railways, and/or airports are unlikely to constitute "silver bullets" that will cause a rise, on their own, of the well-being levels in the region, given the relative satisfaction by residents of available infrastructure. Instead, future policy and investment decisions may need to be multidimensional in their scope, hence addressing the low-performing areas of, for example, governance, health, and education.

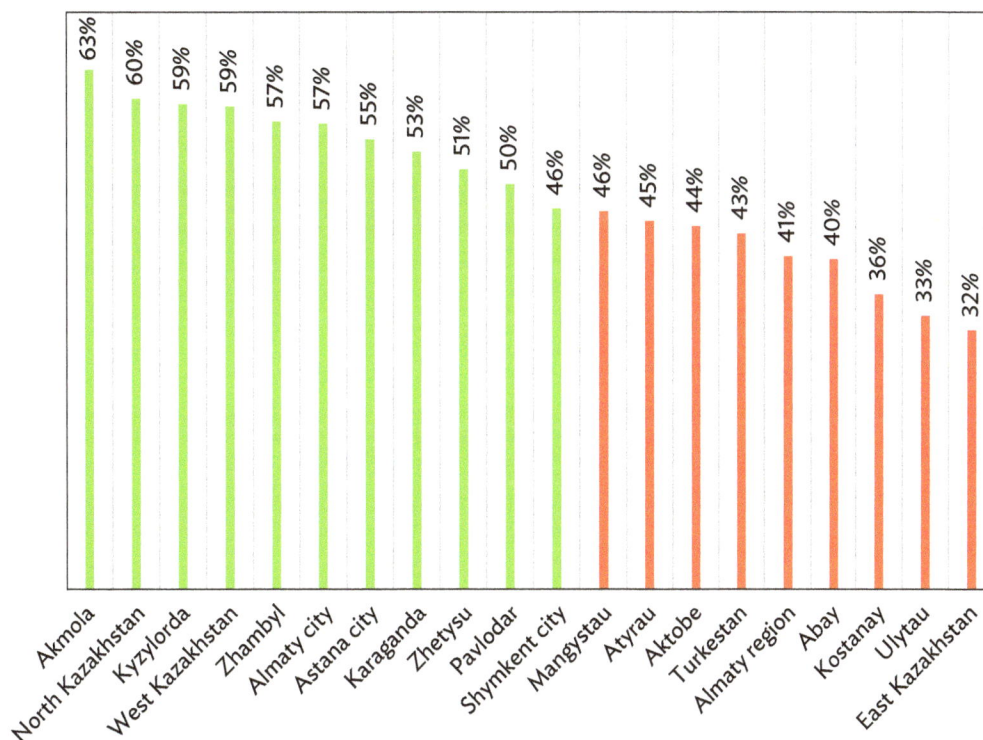

Figure 5: Percentage of Respondents Who Reported Being Satisfied with the Quality of Health Care in Their Region

Source: Authors.

Subjective Well-Being

The last pillar of the SWI is a pure measure of well-being, defined as the combination of life satisfaction and affection. The ranking of Kazakhstan's oblasts according to their performance in the subjective well-being dimension is provided in Table 6. A spatial visualization of the ranking is given in Map 5. At the top of the ranking, we find Almaty city and Shymkent city, together with Atyrau, Karaganda, and Almaty region. In the second quartile, there is a diverse group of oblasts, both western and eastern regions: Kostanay, Zhetysu, Aktobe, East Kazakhstan, and Mangystau. The rest of oblasts are below the national average.

As often described in the literature on well-being, subjective well-being measured through life satisfaction rarely reflects the income distribution, e.g., GDP per capita. In the case of Kazakhstan, we can see this clearly (Figure 6). While there are some regions that display both high GDP per capita levels and high scores in the subjective well-being pillar—Atyrau is a prime example—high scores in the subjective well-being pillar are also enjoyed by oblasts such as Karaganda and Shymkent city that are placed well below on the country's income distribution. In contrast, regions such as West Kazakhstan, which have above-average income levels, perform poorly in the subjective well-being pillar, indicating relatively low levels of satisfaction with life opportunities. In any case, the deviation from the mean is large across the distribution: in regions such as Almaty city and Shymkent city, almost 90% of respondents claim they are satisfied with their life, while in Pavlodar, that figure is 62% and in Abay, 70%. This may point at large differences in living standards, comprising not only material conditions but also social interactions, professional growth opportunities, and the possibility of establishing valuable relationships.

This chapter has illustrated the results of the SWI. As observed, the aggregate scores of the index can be disaggregated by pillar and important insights can be derived from the performance of oblasts on each dimension. The next chapter introduces the Regional Well-Being Index (RWI). This index addresses the need for combining subjective measures of well-being, collected through the countrywide survey, and more objective data related to the same pillars of interest, as a way to obtain a balanced aggregate measure of well-being that can bridge both the picture provided by macro-level, objective indicators and that of well-being perceptions. The next part of the report showcases the methodology of the RWI—which, in many ways, recalls that of the SWI—and the results stemming from the computation of the new index.

Table 6: Ranking of Oblasts on Subjective Well-Being

Rank	Oblast	Normalized Score
1	Almaty city	1.81
2	Atyrau	1.23
3	Shymkent city	1.01
4	Almaty region	1.00
5	Karaganda	0.97
6	Kostanay	0.53
7	Zhetysu	0.48
8	Aktobe	0.46
9	East Kazakhstan	0.22
10	Mangystau	0.17
11	Ulytau	(0.04)
12	Turkestan	(0.20)
13	Akmola	(0.20)
14	Abay	(0.49)
15	North Kazakhstan	(0.53)
16	Astana city	(0.58)
17	West Kazakhstan	(0.65)
18	Kyzylorda	(1.58)
19	Zhambyl	(1.73)
20	Pavlodar	(1.90)

Note: Highlighted from dark green to red are regions according to quartiles of the distribution (e.g., regions highlighted in dark green are in the top quartile).

Source: Authors.

Map 5: Representation of Normalized Scores on Subjective Well-Being, by Oblast

- First quartile
- Second quartile
- Third quartile
- Fourth quartile

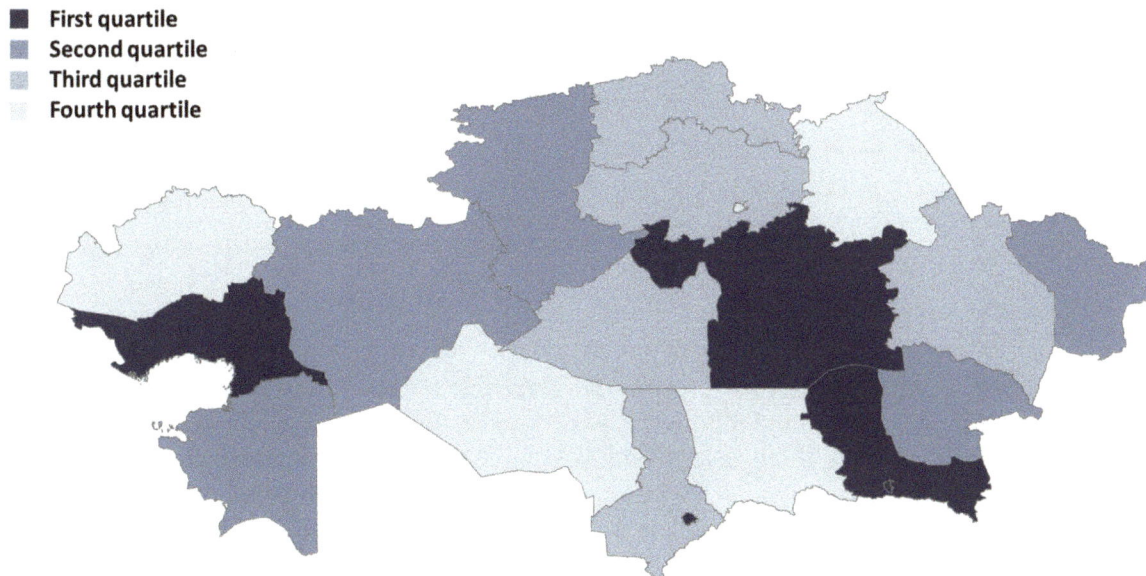

Source: Authors.

Figure 6: Percentage of People Claiming They Are Satisfied with Their Life

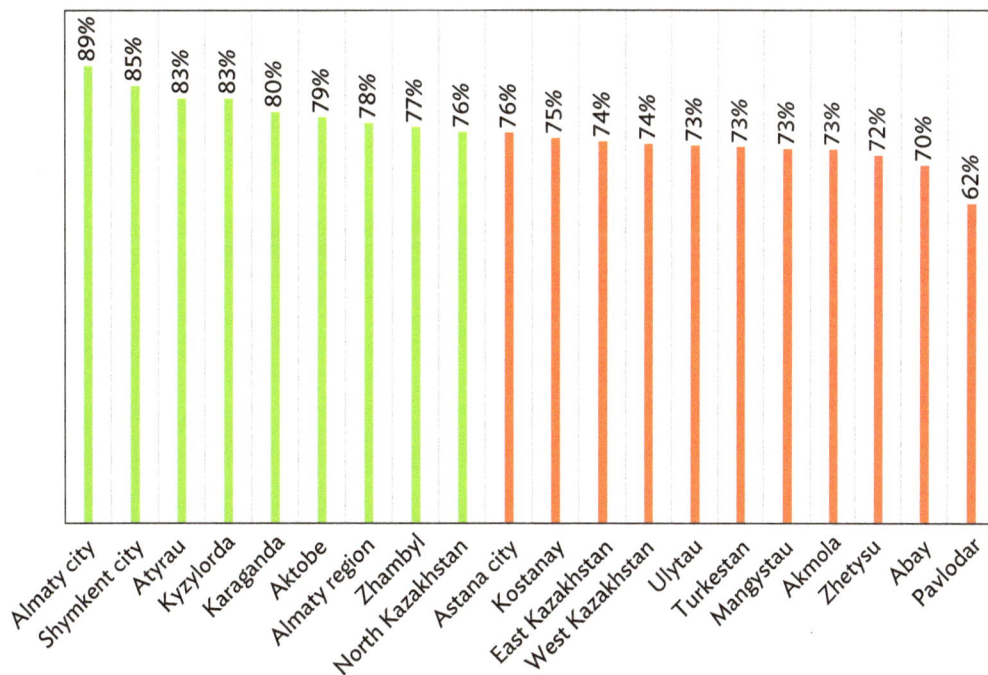

Almaty city	Shymkent city	Atyrau	Kyzylorda	Karaganda	Aktobe	Almaty region	Zhambyl	North Kazakhstan	Astana city	Kostanay	East Kazakhstan	West Kazakhstan	Ulytau	Turkestan	Mangystau	Akmola	Zhetysu	Abay	Pavlodar
89%	85%	83%	83%	80%	79%	78%	77%	76%	76%	75%	74%	74%	73%	73%	73%	73%	72%	70%	62%

Source: Authors.

3 THE REGIONAL WELL-BEING INDEX

3.1 The Methodology for the Regional Well-Being Index

After considering the scores of the SWI, we introduce another measure of well-being, the RWI. The RWI displays several similarities and differences with the SWI. Both indices aim at assessing levels of well-being across Kazakhstan, going beyond hard economic measures of socioeconomic prosperity such as GDP. The methodology behind the construction of the RWI largely recalls the computation techniques employed for the SWI. In practice, this means that the RWI is built upon 10 pillars, and averages are calculated to find an aggregate score that can be used for comparative purposes across oblasts. Both indices introduce novel data on subjective well-being in Kazakhstan; hence, they differentiate themselves significantly from existing measures of prosperity across the population of Kazakhstan.

Figure 7 illustrates the 10 pillars that correspond to the sub-dimensions of the RWI. Like the SWI, the RWI is built around three key headline dimensions—material conditions, quality of life, and subjective well-being. Appendix 3 has more details on the RWI. In practice, the RWI includes the same indicators already present in the SWI, while also incorporating a new set of macro-level variables sourced

Figure 7: Schematic Representation of the Pillars of the Regional Well-Being Index for Kazakhstan

Index of Regional Well-Being of Kazakhstan

Material Conditions	Quality of Life	Subjective Well-Being
Pillar 1. Income and wealth	Pillar 4. Health status	Pillar 10. Subjective well-being
Pillar 2. Work and job quality	Pillar 5. Knowledge and skills	
Pillar 3. Housing conditions	Pillar 6. Social connections and work–life balance	
	Pillar 7. Environmental quality	
	Pillar 8. Civic engagement and governance	
	Pillar 9. Personal security	

Source: Authors.

from Kazakhstan Statistical Office. In this sense, the RWI is a comprehensive assessment of both perceptions (collected through the survey) and outputs of public services. Best practice, such as the OECD Better Life Index, informs the construction of the index, to ensure that the index is consistent with both the theoretical understanding of well-being and the most robust empirical computation techniques. The aggregation techniques, such as the score normalization procedure, reflect the one adopted for the SWI (section 2.3).

3.2   Findings

Overall Scores

This section of the report showcases the results stemming from the computation of the RWI. Table 7 and Map 6 show the ranking of Kazakhstan's oblasts according to their scores on the RWI. Similar to what has been done for the SWI, normalized z-scores are reported in order to facilitate comparison across oblasts. Unlike the SWI, the RWI adopts the pre-2022 classification of the 17 oblasts due to the unavailability of some macro-level indicators. In the first quartile of the distribution, we find North Kazakhstan, Atyrau, Aktobe, Shymkent city, and Astana city. These are followed by Almaty city, Karaganda, Shymkent city, and Mangystau, which are all above the country average. Zhambyl, Pavlodar, Kyzylorda, and Turkestan, which lie at the bottom of the distribution, represent the lowest levels of well-being across the country.

Table 7: Ranking of Kazakhstan's Oblasts in the Regional Well-Being Index

Rank	Oblast	Regional Well-Being Index
1	North Kazakhstan	0.27
2	Atyrau	0.26
3	Aktobe	0.19
4	Astana city	0.14
5	Almaty city	0.14
6	Karaganda	0.11
7	Shymkent city	0.11
8	Mangystau	0.02
9	Almaty region	(0.01)
10	East Kazakhstan	(0.04)
11	West Kazakhstan	(0.05)
12	Kostanay	(0.12)
13	Akmola	(0.14)
14	Turkestan	(0.18)
15	Kyzylorda	(0.24)
16	Pavlodar	(0.27)
17	Zhambyl	(0.41)

( ) = negative.
Note: Highlighted from dark green to red are regions according to quartiles of the distribution (e.g., regions highlighted in dark green are in the top quartile).
Source: Authors.

Map 6: Representation of Normalized Scores of the Regional Well-Being Index

- First quartile
- Second quartile
- Third quartile
- Fourth quartile

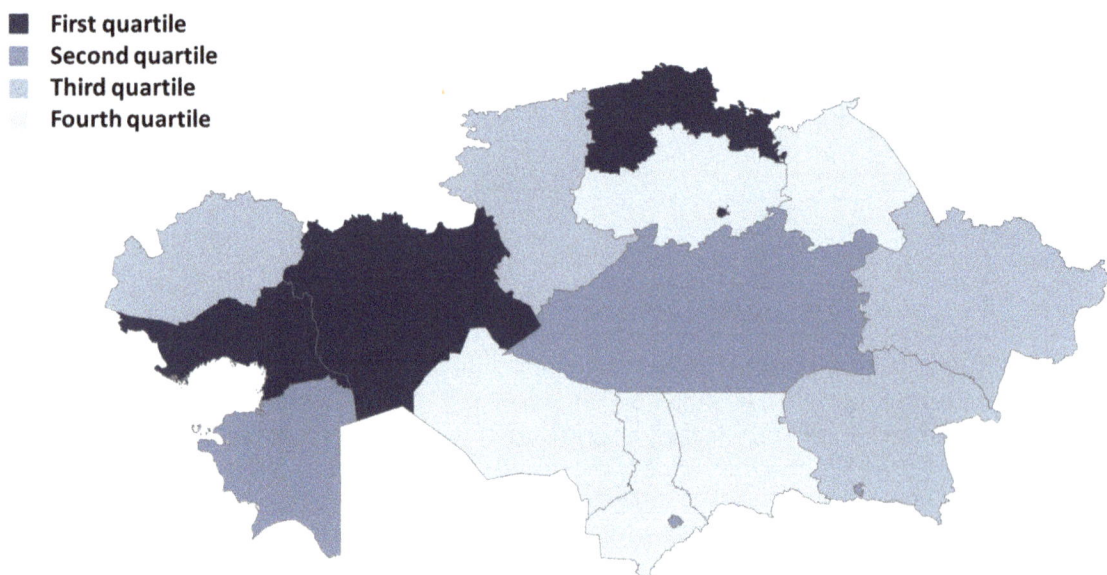

Source: Authors.

A first look at the scores of the RWI reveals a different picture than the one presented by the scores of the SWI. For comparison terms, Table 8 illustrates the rankings of Kazakhstan's oblasts in the two indices. The majority of regions fall in the same half of the distribution in both indices; that is, if an oblast has an above-average score in the SWI, it is likely to be above average also in the RWI. That said, there are a few notable exceptions. For instance, Almaty region appears in the top quartile of the SWI, ranking fourth. Once more objective, macro-level indicators are added to the index specification, however, Almaty region falls to the ninth position, placing it just below the country average on the RWI. Another exception is that of the capital city, Astana. Astana city performs much better once macro-level indicators, such as household disposable income, poverty levels, health status, and educational attainment, enter the formula of the RWI. In contrast, when only people's perceptions are considered, Astana city falls to the bottom of the ranking. Such differences, however, should not be easily dismissed. Low levels of subjective well-being can indeed be the source of social unrest, which if not adequately addressed, may lead to the emergence of violent manifestation of discontent, even though the more objective indicators point to a more positive situation.

Table 8: Comparison of Oblasts' Rankings in the Regional Well-Being Index and the Subjective Well-Being Index

Rank	Regional Well-Being Index	Subjective Well-Being Index
1	North Kazakhstan	Karaganda
2	Atyrau	North Kazakhstan
3	Aktobe	Atyrau
4	Astana city	Almaty region
5	Almaty city	Almaty city
6	Karaganda	Aktobe
7	Shymkent city	Shymkent city
8	Mangystau	Kostanay
9	Almaty region	Akmola
10	East Kazakhstan	Mangystau
11	West Kazakhstan	West Kazakhstan
12	Kostanay	East Kazakhstan
13	Akmola	Turkestan
14	Turkestan	Astana city
15	Kyzylorda	Kyzylorda
16	Pavlodar	Pavlodar
17	Zhambyl	Zhambyl

Note: Highlighted from dark green to red are regions according to quartiles of the distribution (e.g., regions highlighted in dark green are in the top quartile). The three additional oblasts under the new classification—Ulytau, Abay, and Zhetysu—have been removed from the ranking of the Subjective Well-Being Index to facilitate the comparison with the Regional Well-Being Index.

Source: Authors.

The three city regions of Almaty, Astana, and Shymkent exhibit scores above the country average. Interestingly, Astana city displays the highest score among the three, followed by Almaty city and Shymkent city. The aggregate scores, however, hide significant differences among the three cities under each dimension. Figure 8 illustrates the performance of the three cities in the 10 dimensions of the RWI. For instance, Shymkent city performs better than the rest in dimensions such as environmental quality, social connections, and civic engagement, while it lags in income and wealth, knowledge and skills, and health. Astana city, on the other hand, has high scores in income and wealth, work and job quality, and personal safety. However, it has low scores in social connections, civic engagement, and governance and, importantly, life satisfaction. Finally, Almaty city performs relatively better in life satisfaction, health and knowledge, and skills, while it lags in work, civic engagement and governance, and life satisfaction. These differences reveal a very heterogeneous scenario and can be fundamental to drive policy actions aimed at addressing the bottlenecks and weaknesses of each of these territories. In Appendix 4, similar spider charts for each oblast are presented. The following sections introduce individual scores under the three headline categories of the index—material conditions, quality of life, and subjective well-being.

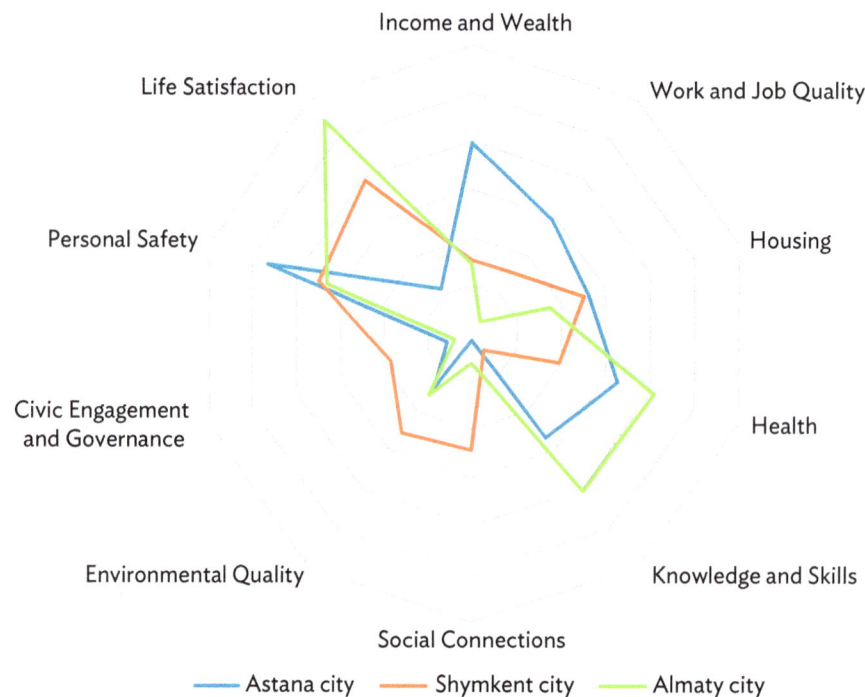

Figure 8: Dimensional Scores of Almaty City, Astana City, and Shymkent City

Source: Authors.

Material Conditions

The material conditions headline dimension of the RWI considers some macro-level economic indicators such as household disposable income and poverty rates. This makes the scores significantly different from those under the same dimension in the SWI. At the top of the ranking in Table 9 we find Karaganda, Astana city, Kyzylorda, and Atyrau. Yet, we can observe how the ranking does not recall exactly the income distribution of Kazakhstan's oblasts, since half of the final score is still computed with perceptions coming from the survey, e.g., data on making ends meet and satisfaction with financial situation (Appendix 2 has the full details). Above the country average, we find many western and northern oblasts such as Aktobe, North Kazakhstan, Mangystau, and Kostanay (Map 7). In contrast, Turkestan, East Kazakhstan, Pavlodar, Zhambyl, and Almaty region lie at the bottom of the distribution, indicating both low satisfaction with the financial situation and low levels of wealth.

Table 9: Ranking of Oblasts on Material Conditions in the Regional Well-Being Index

Rank	Oblast	Normalized Score
1	Karaganda	1.05
2	Astana city	0.90
3	Kyzylorda	0.48
4	Atyrau	0.43
5	Aktobe	0.31
6	North Kazakhstan	0.24
7	Mangystau	0.04
8	Kostanay	0.03
9	West Kazakhstan	(0.10)
10	Akmola	(0.18)
11	Shymkent city	(0.23)
12	Almaty city	(0.28)
13	Almaty region	(0.37)
14	Zhambyl	(0.38)
15	Pavlodar	(0.40)
16	East Kazakhstan	(0.77)
17	Turkestan	(0.77)

Note: Highlighted from dark green to red are regions according to quartiles of the distribution (e.g., regions highlighted in dark green are in the top quartile).
Source: Authors.

Map 7: Representation of Regional Well-Being Scores in the Material Conditions Headline Dimension

■ First quartile
■ Second quartile
■ Third quartile
■ Fourth quartile

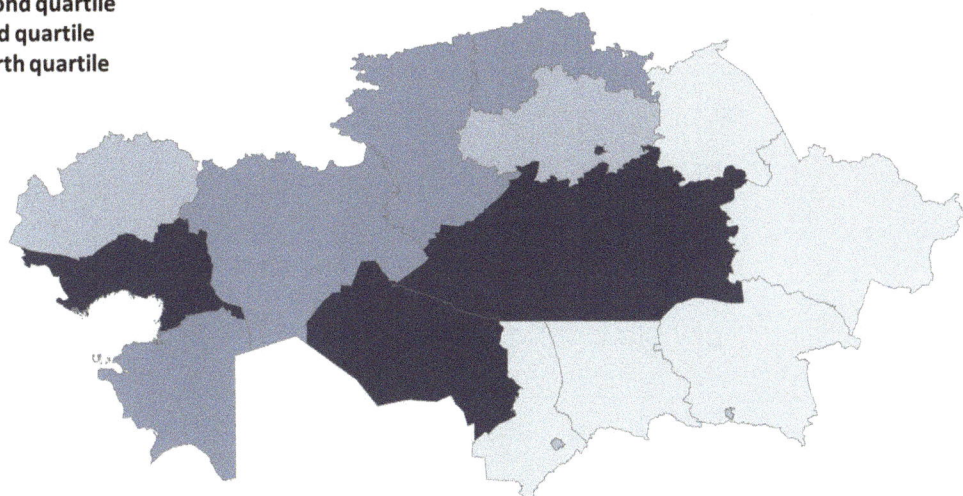

Source: Authors.

Quality of Life

As mentioned in the introductory section, well-being can seldom be captured by purely economic measures. Instead, it is often considered as a multidimensional concept that incorporates other aspects of people's lives, such as health, education, social connections, and civic engagement. Table 10 and Map 8 illustrate the performance of Kazakhstan's oblasts in the quality of life headline dimension. It is interesting to note that some oblasts perform very well under the material conditions headline, yet they lie below the country average in the quality of life dimension. For instance, Karaganda tops the ranking on material conditions, but ranks only 13th on quality of life. In contrast, East Kazakhstan lies at the bottom of the distribution in the material conditions dimension, yet it performs much better once a variety of factors, such as civic engagement and education, are considered. This points, once again, to the importance of going beyond purely economic measures of well-being and collecting data on alternative measures that can inform the actions of policymakers aimed at addressing the bottlenecks of specific territories.

Table 10: Ranking of Oblasts according to Quality of Life in the Regional Well-Being Index

Rank	Oblast	Normalized Score
1	North Kazakhstan	0.38
2	Aktobe	0.15
3	Astana city	0.14
4	Atyrau	0.13
5	Shymkent city	0.05
6	West Kazakhstan	0.03
7	East Kazakhstan	0.03
8	Mangystau	0.01
9	Almaty city	0.01
10	Pavlodar	(0.06)
11	Almaty region	(0. 08)
12	Turkestan	(0.11)
13	Karaganda	(0.10)
14	Akmola	(0.13)
15	Kyzylorda	(0.17)
16	Kostanay	(0.21)
17	Zhambyl	(0.26)

Note: Highlighted from dark green to red are regions according to quartiles of the distribution (e.g., regions highlighted in dark green are in the top quartile).

Source: Authors.

Map 8: Representation of Regional Well-Being Scores in the Quality of Life Headline Dimension

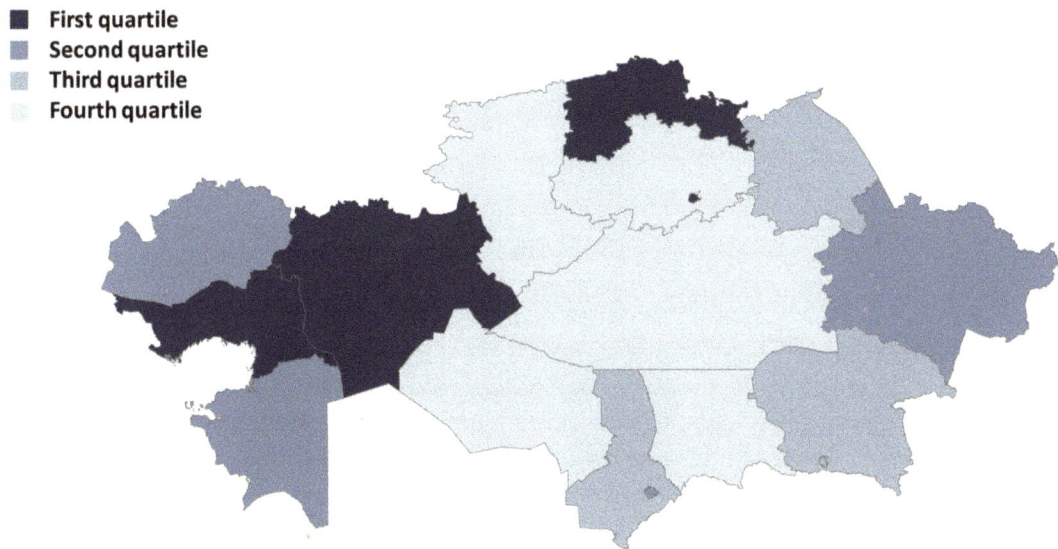

Source: Authors.

Subjective Well-Being

The subjective well-being headline dimension of the RWI is the same as the one presented for the SWI. In Appendix 2, the dimension score is computed by averaging survey responses related to life satisfaction and affection. The ranking of Kazakhstan's oblasts for this pillar can be found in Table 6 and Map 5.

4 POLICY IMPLICATIONS

The study of regional well-being across Kazakhstan's oblasts has emphasized non-negligible differences across the country. The evidence stemming from the report confirms that where people reside plays a role in determining their well-being. Relatedly, enhancing living standards across Kazakhstan requires making where people live a better place. In this context, research on well-being can assist policymakers in directing resources toward those determinants that shape socioeconomic living outcomes in each oblast to a greater extent. Policies capable of better targeting obstacles that curtail improvements in regional well-being are also likely to be more effective and efficient, hence maximizing the social economic returns of the government's development strategies. We present four actionable policy recommendations that are directly derived from our study.

National policies need to provide guidelines, together with an overall vision, but adequate leeway for policy implementation related to regional well-being needs to be granted at the subnational level.

Addressing low well-being levels requires a whole-of-government approach at diverse levels of governance. Policies targeting well-being levels, moreover, cannot be seen as mono-dimensional since the very nature of well-being, as captured by the RWI, spans across different dimensions. In turn, this means that those policies are likely to involve a large number of government offices and ministries, from the economy and education, to health and justice. The number of stakeholders involved, together with the breadth and depth of the expertise required, often makes the development of such policies a challenging undertaking. Quick fixes acting on single dimensions of regional well-being are also unlikely to significantly boost living standards in any given territory.

Similarly, expecting that the development policies needed to improve well-being levels will be homogeneous across different regions is unrealistic. Each region draws from specific sets of strengths and advantages to address its critical dimensions in the RWI. For this reason, while the complexity of regional policies calls for the provision of guidelines by the central government, regions should be given a degree of leeway in the choices pertaining to the implementation of such policies. For instance, in the case of the EU Cohesion Policy and the Smart Specialization strategies, regions are given adequate room to propose in which sectors and how they intend to boost innovation and growth in their regional economies. Regions must also announce up front what objectives they intend to achieve with the available resources and identify precisely how they will measure progress toward those goals. This allows regular monitoring and debate on how financial resources are used. It also means additional funds can be made available to better-performing programs (through a so-called "performance reserve") toward the end of the period (European Commission 2013). However, this does not mean delegating all decisions regarding implementation to oblasts. Whenever necessary, Kazakhstan's central government can ask to modify the implementation of regional policies aimed at improving well-being to ensure coherence with national strategies and support key structural reforms—in the context of the EU Cohesion Policy, the so-called macroeconomic conditionality clause.

Regional targets by the central government should be defined according to an oblast's well-being levels, ideally with the involvement of local stakeholders.

Establishing well-being targets and related key performance indicators against which regions are evaluated and monitored needs to consider the regional differences in well-being levels. The risk of failing to acknowledge the uneven starting points of regions in terms of well-being may lead to the development of targets that are either unrealistic or perceived as a non-priority matter in case they require limited changes to the status quo.

The creation of collaborative policy-making groups when setting well-being targets can increase buy-in from local and regional stakeholders who, depending on the level of political and fiscal decentralization, may be responsible for the implementation of regional strategies aimed at improving well-being levels in their oblasts. Local and regional stakeholders, moreover, usually have an information advantage over government representatives at the central level; hence, involving them in the establishment of realistic well-being targets can effectively tap into their localized expertise (Boschma 2014). In this regard, participatory governance structures, such as interministerial and central–regional committees, will be needed for the development of shared goals and targets.

Conditional funding needs to be allocated to tackle key deficiencies in regional well-being. To do so, Kazakhstan's fiscal redistribution system needs to ensure that regional well-being levels are part of funding allocation decisions.

Devolving authority and tasks to the subnational level to address deficiencies in well-being may lead to unfunded mandates. Unfunded mandates occur when the devolution of responsibilities to regions does not match the devolution of financial resources (Rodriguez-Pose, Tijmstra, and Bwire 2009; Rodríguez-Pose and Vidal-Bover 2022); hence, this creates a scenario where regional governments are unable to meet the objectives for which they are responsible. Just as it is important to build capacity for the implementation of policies that aim to improve well-being levels, the multidimensionality of such policies also calls for substantial financial resources.

An effective way to avoid a scenario of unfunded mandates could consist of incorporating regional scores of well-being into the decision-making process of fiscal redistribution in Kazakhstan. In this way, the central government could ensure it allocates an appropriate portion of subnational funding to the regions where well-being is lowest. By doing so, the mandate of regional governments to address deficiencies in specific areas of standards of living, be it in education, health, personal safety, or environmental quality, can be matched with a suitable and workable financial endowment.

In practice, this can be operationalized by adding the RWI into a formula-based redistribution system, to complement traditional variables that normally enter these types of formulas: demographic and geo-topographic indicators. While investment planning decisions at the regional level are unlikely to draw entirely—or principally—from people's well-being perception, a weighted formula that incorporates, for instance, population size and density, age structure and urbanization, together with the RWI, can lead to the establishment of a balanced fiscal redistribution system for Kazakhstan.

A system of minimum standards that focuses on outcomes, in addition to outputs, could help ensure equitable growth within Kazakhstan. Actions should also be taken to strengthen institutional capacity at the regional level.

The report has highlighted the difference between measuring outputs, or inputs, of public goods and services, and measuring outcomes of well-being. For instance, the regional health expenditure (input) or the number of hospitals (output) can fail to capture people's self-perceived health status or overall satisfaction with health systems (outcomes). At the same time, according to international evidence, outcomes are just as—and sometimes more—important as indicators of the standard of living of the local population (OECD 2013). Even in our study, we found that many higher-income regions display low levels of well-being across the dimensions captured by the index.

A way to limit potential discrepancies that may originate when capturing outputs or outcomes is to establish a system of minimum regional standards that incorporates both. Kazakhstan already possesses a System of Regional Standards that establishes quotas and minimum outputs when it comes to several public services, including the number of hospitals and schools that should be present in every oblast. Such a system can be expanded to include well-being outcomes, as well as complemented by a formula-based redistribution system that allocates funds according to regional scores in the RWI, as proposed earlier.

Finally, proactive measures need to be in place to ensure that regional governments retain enough capacity—beyond financial resources—to implement policies aimed at reaching minimum well-being levels. The institutional capacity of both the implementing agency and local administration assumes increasing relevance when hefty fund transfers are bestowed on regional governments. There is now widespread evidence that local institutional quality matters for development in general, and more specifically for the efficient allocation of resources (Crescenzi and Rodriguez-Pose 2011). Contextually, decentralization has proven most effective in delivering development gains when regional governments are not only given the fiscal resources to implement policy interventions, but they also possess the technical capacity to do so (Rodríguez-Pose and Muštra 2022). Against this backdrop, it is unlikely that the mere transfer of funds from the central government to oblasts will significantly reduce the gaps in living standards across regions in Kazakhstan, even if the redistribution system is rooted in solid formula-based systems. Instead, more holistic intervention that combines the devolution of fiscal resources and the development of institutional capacity at the local level—through, for instance, public secondments and training programs—can deliver greater results for a more equitable Kazakhstan.

5 > CONCLUSIONS

The study of regional inequalities in Kazakhstan is assuming greater and greater importance following the trend of growing territorial imbalances of, at least, the last 4 years (ADB 2021). Previous studies have highlighted the extent and persistence of these inequalities; however, little has been said on the nature and the more qualitative features of regions' different performance across indices' pillars. This report has benchmarked the nature and features of inequalities between Kazakhstan's oblasts through the analysis of a new dataset of primary data stemming from a countrywide survey.

The analysis presented here suggests a multifaceted scenario that can hardly be reconciled with traditional blanket development interventions. Such incongruence arises from how each oblast and territory is characterized by specific strengths and weaknesses, ranging from income levels to health care and education quality. The case of the city region of Astana, for instance, is representative of such eclectic panorama. Astana performed well in the overall scores of the RWI once a range of macro-level, objective indicators were taken into account. That said, residents in Astana expressed little satisfaction with the levels of health care and education provided in the city. Additionally, the city performed very poorly on social connections and work–life balance. This poor performance in these indicators contributed to Astana's low scores in well-being aggregate measures.

The single main takeaway from the analysis carried out on well-being across Kazakhstan's oblasts is that no region is alike, and each region has its own set of challenges and areas for improvement on well-being and living standards. This has major implications for policymakers. Attempts to address regional shortcomings through countrywide blanket policies, such as through the implementation of large infrastructural investments or the establishment of minimum quota systems for the provision of public services, may fail to raise the living standards of all regions. Instead, a much more articulated and demanding undertaking is likely to be needed to design tailored policy interventions that truly address the most pressing issues that persist in Kazakhstan's territories, along the lines of the policy recommendations presented in the previous chapter. In this sense, the adoption of place-sensitive policies could be an important step forward toward the fulfillment of the economic potential of each region, as discussed in ADB (2021).

In practice, regions' SWI and RWI scores can inform a wide range of policies and redistribution allocations. One example is that of fiscal redistribution policies, that is, the transfer of resources from the central to the regional governments. For most parts, current systems of redistribution in Kazakhstan consider output measures of public services determined by the needs of a certain oblast due to, for instance, population density or age. The scores in the two indices presented here, instead, can serve as important outcome indicators of the quality of public goods and services offered, indicating those territories in greater need of resources. Scores can enter formula-based redistribution systems and be part of the rationale for decisions regarding fiscal equalization.

The risks of overlooking low levels of satisfaction with both social and economic outcomes are high. Worldwide, the growing regional imbalances and related discontent that has characterized lagging-behind and declining territories has been a major source of political and social unrest, at times leading to violent manifestation of dissatisfaction such as in the case of the "yellow vests" movement in France. In the past, Kazakhstan has also seen a rise in social discontent that cannot be entirely ascribed to the lack of economic means. Indeed, other factors related to socioeconomic well-being are often the root cause of such unrest, possibly so also in the case of Kazakhstan. For instance, the 2022 violent unrest in the country sparked from the oil-rich, high-income region of Mangystau. All this calls for renewed attention to different levels of well-being across Kazakhstan's oblasts, and a deep understanding of what drives those levels of satisfaction (or discontent). This focus and understanding will help policymakers design and implement targeted actions that will contribute to a more equitable, inclusive, and sustainable Kazakhstan.

QUESTIONNAIRE FOR THE MEASUREMENT OF REGIONAL WELL-BEING IN KAZAKHSTAN

MODULE 1: Demographic questions

This module collects information related to the demographic information of the respondent.

Q1 Respondent's sex (Code respondent's sex by observation, don't ask about it):

1   Male

2   Female

Q2 Year of birth ....

or

Q2 To which age group do you belong?

- 15–29 years old
- 30–44 years old
- 45–64 years old
- 65 and +
- Prefer not to answer

Q3 Were you born in this country or are you an immigrant to this country?

Q4 Are you currently (read out and code one answer only):

1   Married

2   Divorced

3   Separated

4   Widowed

5   Single

Q5 Do you have any children? (Code 0 if no, and respective number if yes):

Q6 In which oblast do you reside?

....

Q7 Do you live in the oblast you were born?

....

MODULE 2: Core measures of subjective well-being

The following module is intended to provide a minimal set of measures of subjective well-being covering both life evaluations and affection that could be included in household surveys. The core measures included here are the measures for which there is the strongest evidence for their validity and relevance, and for which international comparability is the most important.

Q8 Overall, how satisfied are you with life as a whole these days? [0-10]

Please imagine a ladder with steps numbered from zero at the bottom to 10 at the top. Suppose we say that the top of the ladder represents the best possible life for you and the bottom of the ladder represents the worst possible life for you. If the top step is 10 and the bottom step is 0, on which step of the ladder do you feel you personally stand at the present time?

0   1   2   3   4   5   6   7   8   9   10

Q9 Overall, to what extent do you feel the things you do in your life are worthwhile? [0-10]

The following question asks how worthwhile you feel the things you do in your life are, on a scale from 0 to 10. Zero means you feel the things you do in your life are "not at all worthwhile", and 10 means "completely worthwhile."

0   1   2   3   4   5   6   7   8   9   10

Q10 The following questions ask about how you felt yesterday on a scale from 0 to 10. Zero means you did not experience the feeling "at all" while 10 means you experienced the feeling "all of the time." I will now read out a list of ways you might have felt yesterday.

How about happy? [0-10]

0   1   2   3   4   5   6   7   8   9   10

How about worried? [0-10]

0   1   2   3   4   5   6   7   8   9   10

How about depressed? [0-10]

0   1   2   3   4   5   6   7   8   9   10

How about well-rested? [0-10]

0   1   2   3   4   5   6   7   8   9   10

Module 3: Material conditions
The following module covers variables related to material conditions such as income, jobs, housing.

Q11 What is your household income?

....

Or include a scale range based on the average income for Kazakhstan

Q12 Do you have difficulty in making ends meet?

Yes [1]
No [0]

Q13 How satisfied are you with the financial situation of your household? [0-10]

0   1   2   3   4   5   6   7   8   9   10

Q14 Comparing your standard of living with your parents' standard of living when they were about your age, would you say that you are better off, worse off, or about the same?

1 Worse off

2 About the same

3 Better off

Q15 How many hours do you work, on average, per week?

.... Hours

Or include a range of hours

Q16 How likely are you to work overtime?

Never [1]
Rarely [2]
Frequently [3]
Always [4]

Q17 Overall, how satisfied are you with your job?

Very satisfied [4]
Satisfied [3]
Not so satisfied [2
Not satisfied at all [1]

Q18 Are you satisfied with the job opportunities available in your area?

Yes [1]
No [0]

Q19 How likely would your colleagues be to give you work-related help or advice, if needed?

Not likely at all [1]
Not very likely [2]
Likely [3]
Very likely [4]

Q20 Overall, how satisfied are you with your housing situation?

Very satisfied [4]
Satisfied [3]
Not so satisfied [2]
Not satisfied at all [1]

Q21 What percentage of your income goes toward rent/housing costs?

... %

Or include a range

Module 4: Quality of Life
The following module covers variables related to quality of life.

Section 4.1: Social capital, civic engagement and governance

Q22 Generally speaking, would you say that most people can be trusted or that you need to be very careful in dealing with people? (Code one answer):

Most people can be trusted [2]

Need to be very careful [1]

Q23 I am going to name a number of organizations. For each one, could you tell me how much confidence you have in them: a great deal of confidence [4], quite a lot of confidence [3], not very much confidence [2], or none at all [1]? (Read out and code one answer for each):

The police	1	2	3	4
The courts	1	2	3	4
The government	1	2	3	4
The armed forces	1	2	3	4
The press	1	2	3	4
Television	1	2	3	4
Labor unions	1	2	3	4
Political parties	1	2	3	4
Parliament	1	2	3	4
The civil service	1	2	3	4
Universities	1	2	3	4
Elections	1	2	3	4
Major companies	1	2	3	4
Banks	1	2	3	4
Environmental organizations	1	2	3	4

Q24 How would you place your views on corruption in your country on a 10-point scale where "0" means "there is no corruption in my country" and "10" means "there is abundant corruption in my country."

0   1   2   3   4   5   6   7   8   9   10

Q25 How often do you think ordinary people like yourself have to pay a bribe, give a gift or do a favor to these people in order to get the services you need? Does it happen never, rarely, frequently, or always?

Never [1]

Rarely [2]

Frequently [3]

Always [4]

Q26 How high is the risk in this region to be held accountable for giving or receiving a bribe, gift, or favor in return for public service? To indicate your opinion, use a 10-point scale where "1" means "no risk at all" and "10" means "very high risk."

0   1   2   3   4   5   6   7   8   9   10

Q27 How interested would you say you are in politics? Are you (read out and code one answer):

Not at all interested [1]

Not very interested [2]

Somewhat interested [3]

Very interested [4]

Q28 How much would you say the political system in your country allows people like you to have a say in what the government does?

A great deal [5]

A lot [4]

Some [3]

Very little [2]

Not at all [1]

Section 4.2: Social connections and work–life balance

Q29 If you were in trouble, do you have relatives or friends you can count on to help you whenever you need them, or not?

Yes [1]

No [0]

Q30 Overall, are you satisfied with the personal relationships in your life? Please make a broad, reflective appraisal of all areas of his/her personal relationships (e.g., relatives, friends, colleagues from work, etc.).

Yes [1]

No [0]

Q31 How often do you meet socially with friends, relatives, or work colleagues?

Never [1]

Rarely [2]

Frequently [3]

Always [4]

Q32 Overall, are you satisfied with your time use?

Yes [1]

No [0]

Section 4.3: Health and education

Q33 How is your health in general?

Very good [4]

Good [3]

Not so good [2]

Poor [1]

Q34 Are you hampered in your daily activities in any way by any long-standing illness, or disability, infirmity or mental health problem?

Yes [1]

No [0]

Q35 Are you satisfied with the level of health care available in your area?

Yes [1]

No [0]

Q36 Do you think there are enough hospitals in your area?

Yes [1]

No [0]

Q37 What is your level of education?

Primary [1]

Secondary [2]

Tertiary/university [3]

Q38 Are you satisfied with the education you received?

Yes [1]

No [0]

Q39 Do you think there are enough schools in your area?

Yes [1]

No [0]

Q40 Do you think there are enough universities in your area?

Yes [1]

No [0]

Section 4.4: Environment and natural capital

Q41 How satisfied are you with the environmental quality of your area?

Very satisfied [4]

Satisfied [3]

Not so satisfied [2]

Not satisfied at all [1]

Q42 Do you believe pollution (i.e., air, water, sound) is too high in your area?

Yes [1]

No [0]

Q43 Are you satisfied with the number of public green areas around your house?

Very satisfied [4] Satisfied [3] Not so satisfied [2] Not satisfied at all [1]

Q44 How worried are you about climate change?

Extremely worried [1] Somewhat worried [2] Not very worried [3] Not worried at all [4]

Q45 How satisfied are you about the government action to tackle climate change?

Very satisfied [4] Satisfied [3] Not so satisfied [2] Not satisfied at all [1]

Section 4.5: Personal security

Q46 How safe do you feel walking alone in your area after dark?

Very safe 4

Quite safe 3

Not very secure 2

Not at all secure 1

Q47 Could you tell me how secure do you feel these days?

Very secure 4

Quite secure 3

Not very secure 2

Not at all secure 1

Q48 To what degree are you worried about the following situations? Very much [4] A good deal [3] Not much [2] Not at all [1]

A war involving my country 1 2 3 4

A terrorist attack 1 2 3 4

A civil war 1 2 3 4

Q49 How satisfied are you with the law enforcement in your area?

Very satisfied [4]

Satisfied [3]

Not so satisfied [2]

Not satisfied at all [1]

TECHNICAL METHODOLOGY OF THE REGIONAL WELL-BEING SURVEY FOR KAZAKHSTAN

The sampling of the population was a multistage effort. The first stage consisted of a stratified sampling of the total population of Kazakhstan in each oblast, according to their population share. The volume of strata ranged from 160 to 437 respondents, depending on the population in the regions. The second stage of selection consisted of a stratified selection for cities and villages in each oblast, according to their level of urbanization. Third, nest sampling was adopted, that is, regional centers themselves and other localities were selected for the survey according to the principle of territorial remoteness from the regional center: cities of regional or district significance, villages located near cities, and remote villages. Fourth, to further ensure the representativeness of the sample, the team conducted a quota selection according to age, gender, and ethnic group. With a confidence probability of 95% and a proportion of 50%, the sampling error in the survey of 4,000 respondents was ± 1.55%. The sampling error is calculated according to the formula:

$$\Delta = \pm t \sqrt{\frac{\sigma^2}{n}\left(1 - \frac{n}{N}\right)} * 100\%$$

where
Δ = *sampling error*;
σ^2 = variance of the proportion of feature x in the sample population;
n - sample population;
N - general population;
t - normalized deviation, the "confidence coefficient."

Finally, the questionnaire design was formed considering the respondent's cognitive burden; the time budget of the survey; and the need to produce a questionnaire that is clear, comprehensible, and that flows well across its modules. Question placement can be a crucial factor when setting the design of the questionnaire. Based on the review of best practice, we placed subjective well-being questions at the beginning of the survey, avoiding placing well-being questions immediately after questions which can elicit a strong emotional response (such as questions on income or marital status), making use of transition questions and buffer text to refocus respondent attention (Deaton 2011). Moreover, introductory text can help respondents distinguish between topics. Question order within well-being questions should also be considered. The general rule is to move from the general to the specific (Organisation for Economic Co-operation and Development [OECD] 2013). Core modules should be placed at the beginning, with this normally being a question on the Cantril Ladder self-anchoring striving scale, overall happiness questions, and questions related to affection. The core module usually serves as the primary measure of well-being when a single measure is required. To follow, we introduced domain-specific modules in the questionnaire design. Domain evaluation modules aim to collect people's evaluative judgments on how well various aspects of their life are going. These measures can be summed, and mean scores can be used to calculate a composite index such as the Personal Well-Being Index and Better Life Index developed by the OECD with the support of the main consultant.

INDICATORS FOR THE REGIONAL WELL-BEING INDEX OF KAZAKHSTAN

Pillars		Proposed Indicators	Description	Geographical Level
1. Income and wealth	1.01	Household net disposable income	Maximum amount that a household can afford to consume without having to reduce its assets or to increase its liabilities	Oblast
	1.02	Poverty rates	% of total population living in poverty	Oblast
	1.03	Difficulty making ends meet	% of people who report having difficulty in making ends meet	Oblast
	1.04	Satisfaction with financial situation	% of people reporting they are overall satisfied with their financial situation	Oblast
	1.05	Better living standards than parents	% of people who believe their standards of living are better off than those of their parents when they were about the same age	Oblast
2. Work and job quality	2.01	Employment rate	Persons employed aged 15–64 (excluding agriculture) as % of population same age cohort	Oblast
	2.02	Unemployment rate	% of active population	Oblast
	2.03	Youth unemployment	% of youth out of employment	Oblast
	2.04	Long hours in employment	Share of employees (of all ages) whose usual working hours are 50 hours or more per week	Oblast
	2.05	Satisfaction with job	% of people who report they are satisfied with their job conditions	Oblast
	2.06	Satisfaction with job opportunities	% of people who report being satisfied with job opportunities in their area	Oblast
3. Housing	3.01	Households without basic facilities	% of the population living in a dwelling without indoor flushing toilet for the sole use of their households	Oblast
	3.02	Household access to internet	% of total households	Oblast
	3.03	Satisfaction with housing conditions	% of people who report they are satisfied with their current housing conditions	Oblast

Pillars	Proposed Indicators		Description	Geographical Level
4. Health status	4.01	Life expectancy	Number of years of healthy life expected	Oblast
	4.02	Self-reported health	% of people who report "very good" or "good" health	Oblast
	4.03	Suicide death rate	Standardized death rate for suicide for population under 65	Oblast
	4.04	Satisfaction with health care	% of people who report they are satisfied with the public health care provided	Oblast
	4.05	Health-hampering conditions	% of people who report being hampered in their daily activities in any way by any long-standing illness, disability, infirmity, or mental health problem	Oblast
5. Knowledge and skills	5.01	Educational attainment	Educational attainment considers the number of adults aged 25–64 holding at least an upper secondary degree over the population of the same age	Oblast
	5.02	Student skills	Students' average score in, for instance, reading, mathematics, and science	Oblast
	5.03	Satisfaction with education system	% of people who report they are satisfied with the overall education system	Oblast
6. Social connections	6.01	Social support	% of people answering "yes" to a (yes/no) question: "If you were in trouble, do you have relatives or friends you can count on to help you whenever you need them, or not?	Oblast
	6.02	Social life	% of people who report that they meet "always" or "frequently" with friends, relatives, or work colleagues	Oblast
7. Environmental quality	7.01	Air pollution	Population weighted average of annual concentrations of particulate matters less than 2.5 microns in diameter (PM2.5) in the air	Oblast
	7.02	Satisfaction with environmental quality	% of people reporting they are satisfied with the quality of the environment in their areas	Oblast
	7.03	Satisfaction with green areas	% of people who report they are satisfied with the number of green spaces in their areas	Oblast
	7.04	Climate change concerns	% of people who report they are "extremely concerned" and "concerned" by climate change	Oblast
8. Civic engagement and governance	8.01	Voter turnout	Ratio between the number of individuals that cast a ballot during an election (whether this vote is valid or not) to the population registered to vote	Oblast
	8.02	Trust level	% of people who report people in their area can be trusted	Oblast
	8.03	Confidence in police, courts, and government	% of people who report having confidence in the police, courts, and government	Oblast
	8.04	Perceived corruption	% of people who believe there is high corruption in the country	Oblast
	8.05	Civic participation	% of people who feel they can contribute to the country	Oblast

Pillars	Proposed Indicators		Description	Geographical Level
9. Personal safety	9.01	Homicides	Deaths due to assault (rate per 100,000 population)	Oblast
	9.02	Road fatality	Road deaths (rate per 100,000 population)	Oblast
	9.03	Feeling safe at night	% of residents feeling safe walking at night	Oblast
10. Life satisfaction	10.01	Life satisfaction	% of people overall satisfied with life quality	Oblast
	10.02	Worthwhile life	% of people who feel that they have a worthwhile life	Oblast
	10.03	Negative affect balance	% of respondents who report more negative than positive feelings or states on the previous day	Oblast

OBLASTS' PERFORMANCE IN 10 DIMENSIONS OF THE REGIONAL WELL-BEING INDEX

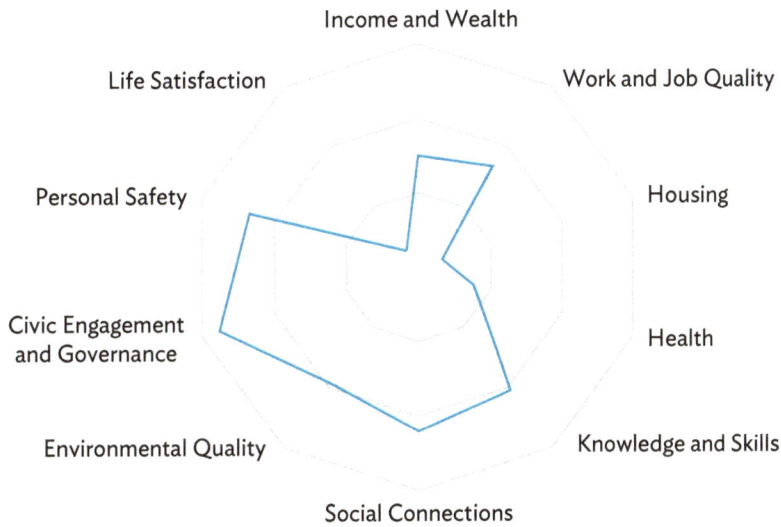

Figure A4.1: North Kazakhstan

Income and Wealth

Life Satisfaction

Work and Job Quality

Personal Safety

Housing

Civic Engagement and Governance

Health

Environmental Quality

Knowledge and Skills

Social Connections

Source: Authors.

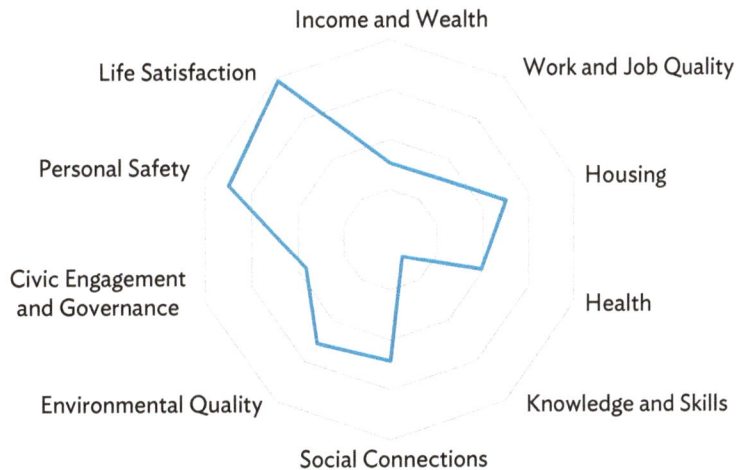

Figure A4.2: Shymkent City

Income and Wealth

Life Satisfaction

Work and Job Quality

Personal Safety

Housing

Civic Engagement and Governance

Health

Environmental Quality

Knowledge and Skills

Social Connections

Source: Authors.

Figure A4.3: Astana City

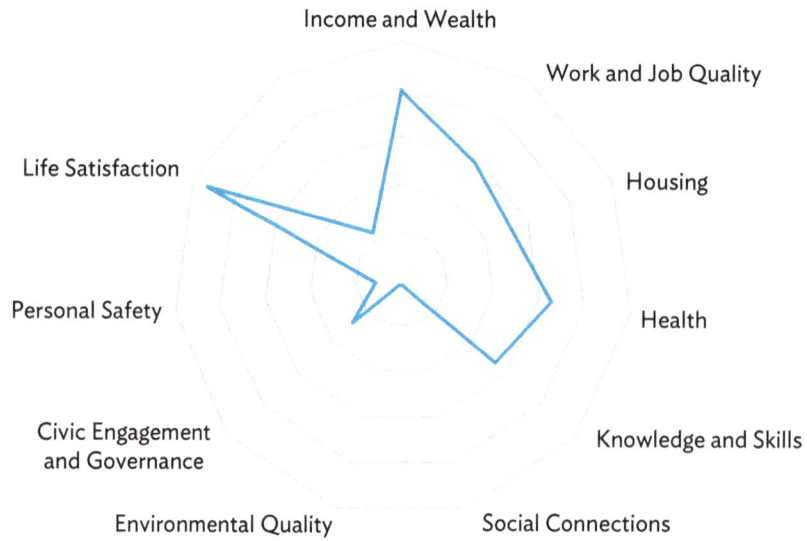

Source: Authors.

Figure A4.4: Atyrau

Source: Authors.

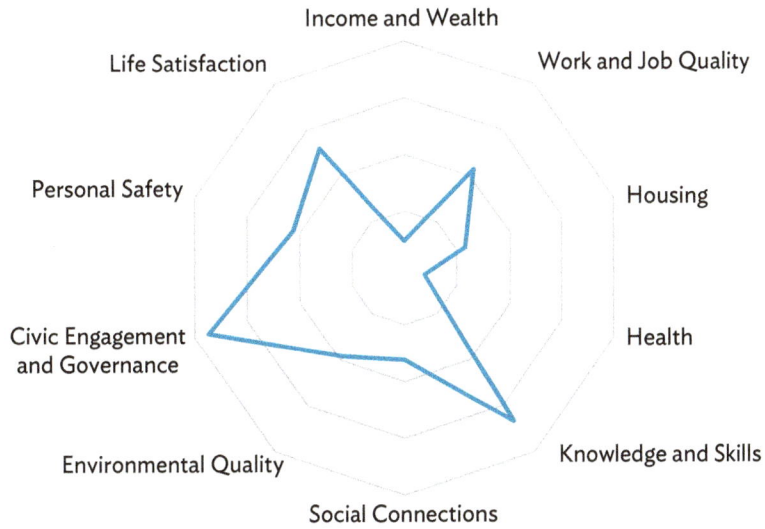

Figure A4.5: East Kazakhstan

Source: Authors.

Figure A4.6: Aktobe

Source: Authors.

Figure A4.7: Mangystau

Income and Wealth

Life Satisfaction

Work and Job Quality

Personal Safety

Housing

Civic Engagement
and Governance

Health

Environmental Quality

Knowledge and Skills

Social Connections

Source: Authors.

Figure A4.8: Pavlodar

Income and Wealth

Life Satisfaction

Work and Job Quality

Personal Safety

Housing

Civic Engagement
and Governance

Health

Environmental Quality

Knowledge and Skills

Social Connections

Source: Authors.

Figure A4.9: Almaty City

Income and Wealth
Life Satisfaction
Work and Job Quality
Personal Safety
Housing
Civic Engagement and Governance
Health
Environmental Quality
Knowledge and Skills
Social Connections

Source: Authors.

Figure A4.10: West Kazakhstan

Income and Wealth
Life Satisfaction
Work and Job Quality
Personal Safety
Housing
Civic Engagement and Governance
Health
Environmental Quality
Knowledge and Skills
Social Connections

Source: Authors.

Figure A4.11: Karaganda

Income and Wealth

Life Satisfaction

Work and Job Quality

Personal Safety

Housing

Civic Engagement
and Governance

Health

Environmental Quality

Knowledge and Skills

Social Connections

Source: Authors.

Figure A4.12: Almaty Region

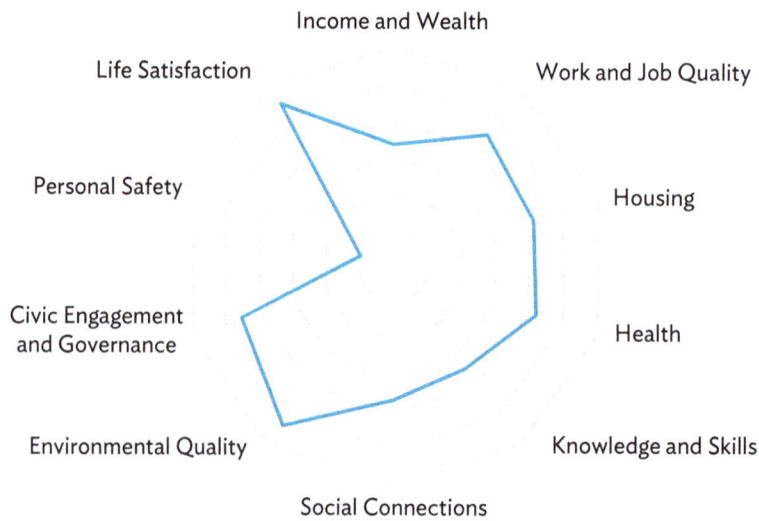

Income and Wealth

Life Satisfaction

Work and Job Quality

Personal Safety

Housing

Civic Engagement
and Governance

Health

Environmental Quality

Knowledge and Skills

Social Connections

Source: Authors.

Figure A4.13: Turkestan

Income and Wealth
Life Satisfaction
Work and Job Quality
Personal Safety
Housing
Civic Engagement and Governance
Health
Environmental Quality
Knowledge and Skills
Social Connections

Source: Authors.

Figure A4.14: Kyzylorda

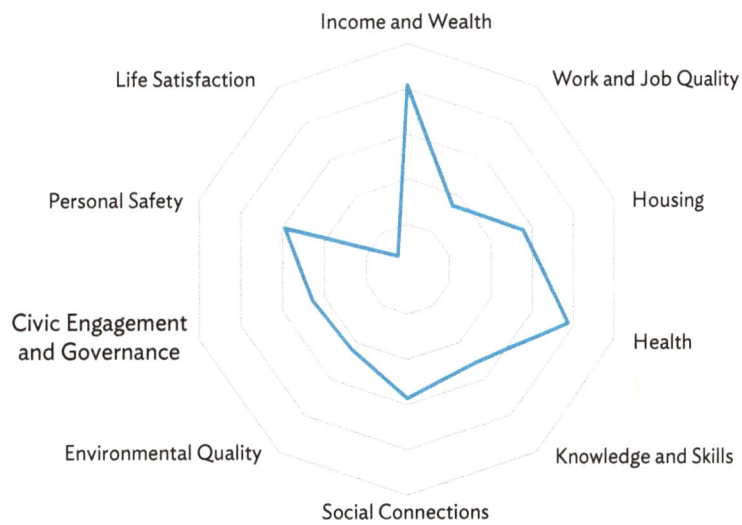

Income and Wealth
Life Satisfaction
Work and Job Quality
Personal Safety
Housing
Civic Engagement and Governance
Health
Environmental Quality
Knowledge and Skills
Social Connections

Source: Authors.

Figure A4.15: Kostanay

Income and Wealth
Work and Job Quality
Housing
Health
Knowledge and Skills
Social Connections
Environmental Quality
Civic Engagement and Governance
Personal Safety
Life Satisfaction

Source: Authors.

Figure A4.16: Zhambyl

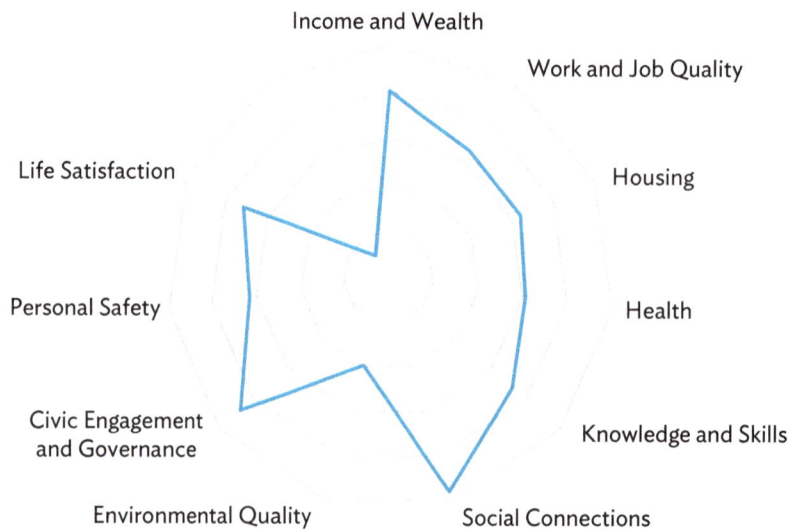

Income and Wealth
Work and Job Quality
Housing
Health
Knowledge and Skills
Social Connections
Environmental Quality
Civic Engagement and Governance
Personal Safety
Life Satisfaction

Source: Authors.

Figure A4.17: Akmola

Income and Wealth

Life Satisfaction

Work and Job Quality

Personal Safety

Housing

Civic Engagement
and Governance

Health

Environmental Quality

Knowledge and Skills

Social Connections

Source: Authors.

REFERENCES

Asian Development Bank (ADB). 2021. *Joint Government of Kazakhstan and the Asian Development Bank, Knowledge and Experience Exchange Program, Phase 4*. Consultant's report. Astana (TA 6623-KAZ).

Boarini, R., M. Comola, C. Smith, R. Manchin, and F. De Keulenaer. 2012. What Makes for a Better Life?: The Determinants of Subjective Well-Being in OECD Countries: Evidence from the Gullap World Poll. *OECD Statistics Working Papers*. No. 2012/03. Paris: Organisation for Economic Co-operation and Development (OECD).

Boschma, R. 2014. Constructing Regional Advantage and Smart Specialisation: Comparison of Two European Policy Concepts. *Scienze Regional*. 13. 51-68.

Clark, A. and C. Senik. 2010. Will GDP Growth Increase Happiness in Developing Countries? In R. Peccoud, ed. *Measure for Measure: How Well Do We Measure Development?* Paris: Agence Française de Développement.

Crescenzi, R. and A. Rodríguez-Pose. 2011. *Innovation and Regional Growth in the European Union*. Springer Science & Business Media.

Deaton, A. S. 2011. The Financial Crisis and the Well-Being of Americans. *NBER Working Paper*. No. 17128. Cambridge, MA: National Bureau of Economic Research (NBER).

Diener, E. 2006. Guidelines for National Indicators of Subjective Well-Being and Ill-Being. *Journal of Happiness Studies: An Interdisciplinary Forum on Subjective Well-Being*. 7 (4). pp. 397–404.

Dolan, P., T. Peasgood, and M. White. 2008. Do We Really Know What Makes Us Happy? A Review of the Economic Literature on the Factors Associated with Subjective Well-Being. *Journal of Economic Psychology*. 29 (1). pp. 94–122.

European Commission. 2013 Refocusing EU Cohesion Policy for Maximum Impact on Growth and Jobs: The Reform in 10 points. 19 November. Brussels, Belgium.

Fan, S., R. Kanbur, and X. Zhang. 2011. China's Regional Disparities: Experience and Policy. *Review of Development Finance*. 1 (1). pp. 47–56.

Fujiwara, D. and R. Campbell. 2011. *Valuation Techniques for Social Cost–Benefit Analysis: Stated Preference, Revealed Preference and Subjective Well-Being Approaches—A Discussion of the Current Issues*. London: HM Treasury.

Gallup. 2011. *Tunisia: Analysing the Dawn of the Arab Spring.* Abu Dhabi: Gallup.

Government of South Africa, National Planning Commission (NPC). 2012. *National Development Plan 2030: Our Future—Make It Work.* Pretoria.

Halpern, D. 2010. *The Hidden Wealth of Nations.* London: Polity.

Helliwell, J. 2008. Life Satisfaction and the Quality of Development. *NBER Working Paper.* No. 14507. Cambridge, MA: NBER.

Helliwell, J. and C. Barrington-Leigh. 2010. Measuring and Understanding Subjective Well-Being. *Canadian Journal of Economics/Revue canadienne d'économique.* 43 (3). pp. 729–753.

Helliwell, J. F. and S. Wang. 2011. Trust and Well-Being. *International Journal of Well-being.* 1 (1).

Huppert, F. 2009. Psychological Well-Being: Evidence Regarding Its Causes and Consequences. *Applied Psychology: Health and Well-Being.* 1 (2). pp. 137–164.

Iammarino, S., A. Rodriguez-Pose, and M. Storper. 2019. Regional Inequality in Europe: Evidence, Theory and Policy Implications. *Journal of Economic Geography.* 19 (2). pp. 273–298.

International Monetary Fund. 2022. *World Economic Outlook Database.* https://www.imf.org/en/Publications/SPROLLs/world-economic-outlook-databases#sort=%40imfdate%20descending (accessed December 2022).

Kahneman, D. and A. Krueger. 2006. Developments in the Measurement of Subjective Well-being. *Journal of Economic Perspectives.* 20 (1). pp. 3–24.

NPC. 2012. National Development Plan 2030: Our future–make it work. Pretoria: Government of South Africa.

OECD. 2011. *How's Life? Measuring Well-Being.* Paris: OECD Publishing.

OECD. 2013. *OECD Guidelines on Measuring Subjective Well-being.* Paris: OECD Publishing.

Oswald, F., H. Wahl, H. Mollenkopf, and O. Schilling, O. 2003. Housing and Life Satisfaction of Older Adults in Two Rural Regions in Germany. *Research on Ageing.* 25 (2). pp. 122–143.

Rodríguez-Pose, A. 2018. The Revenge of the Places That Don't Matter (And What to Do about It). *Cambridge Journal of Regions, Economy and Society.* 11 (1). pp. 189–209.

Rodríguez-Pose, A. and V. Muštra. 2022. The Economic Returns of Decentralisation: Government Quality and the Role of Space. *Environment and Planning A: Economy and Space.* 54 (8). pp. 1604–1622.

Rodríguez-Pose, A., S. A. Tijmstra, and A. Bwire. 2009. Fiscal Decentralisation, Efficiency, and Growth. *Environment and Planning A: Economy and Space.* 41 (9). pp. 2041–2062.

Rodríguez-Pose, A. and M. Vidal-Bover. 2022. Unfunded Mandates and the Economic Impact of Decentralisation. When Finance Does Not Follow Function. *Political Studies*. ISSN 2041-9066.

Ryan, R. M. and E. L. Deci. 2001. To Be Happy or to Be Self-Fulfilled: A Review of Research on Hedonic and Eudaimonic Well-Being. *Annual Review of Psychology*. 52 (1). pp. 141–166.

Stiglitz, J. E. and J. P. Fitoussi. 2009. *Report by the Commission on the Measurement of Economic Performance and Social Progress.*

www.ingramcontent.com/pod-product-compliance
Lightning Source LLC
Chambersburg PA
CBHW050052220326
41599CB00045B/7377